TEACHING
2 TIMOTHY

The Teaching series is a great resource for Bible study leaders and pastors, indeed for any Christian who wants to understand their Bible better.

Mark Dever
Senior Pastor of Capitol Hill Baptist Church and
President of 9Marks, Washington, DC

The task of moving from the text of Scripture to clear and faithful exposition is challenging. This series of excellent guides aims to help the Bible teacher to observe what is there in the text, and prepare to convey its significance to contemporary hearers. In this way these volumes often do more than the weightier technical commentaries. It is like having the guidance of an experienced coach in the wonderful work of rightly handling the word of truth.

John Woodhouse
Retired Principal,
Moore College,
Sydney, Australia

North India desperately needs men and women who will preach and teach the Bible faithfully and PT's Teaching series is of great value in encouraging them to do just that. They are just what we need. We have found the books of great help in English and eagerly anticipate the day when they will be available in Hindi also.

Isaac Shaw
Executive Director,
Delhi Bible Institute

This teaching series, written by skilled and trustworthy students of God's Word, helps us to understand the Bible, believe it and obey it. I commend it to all Bible readers, but especially those whose task it is to teach the inspired Word of God.

Peter Jensen
Former Archbishop of Sydney

TEACHING
2 TIMOTHY

From text to message

JONATHAN GRIFFITHS

SERIES EDITORS: DAVID JACKMAN & ADRIAN REYNOLDS

PT RESOURCES

CHRISTIAN
FOCUS

Jonathan Griffiths serves as tutor on the Cornhill Training Course. He previously served as assistant minister at Christ Church, Westbourne. He is married to Gemma and they have two children, Edward and Arabella.

Copyright © Proclamation Trust Resources 2014

ISBN 978-1-78191-389-5

10 9 8 7 6 5 4 3 2 1

Published in 2014
by
Christian Focus Publications Ltd.,
Geanies House, Fearn, Ross-shire,
IV20 1TW, Scotland, Great Britain.
with
Proclamation Trust Resources,
Willcox House, 140-148 Borough High Street,
London, SE1 1LB, England, Great Britain.
www.proctrust.org.uk

www.christianfocus.com

Cover design by DUFI-ART.com

Printed by
Nørhaven, Denmark

Contents

For my parents
with love and gratitude

Series Preface

Paul's second letter to Timothy is a key New Testament epistle for Bible ministry. Its focus and emphasis have long been a touchstone for the ministry of The Proclamation Trust as we seek to encourage and equip Bible preachers and teachers in the local church. A quick review of the resources on our website (www.proctrust.org.uk) shows that we return to it time and time again to further this cause.

This is therefore an important volume in our *Teaching...* series. Nevertheless, its importance is not – primarily – simply as an instruction manual for preachers or would-be pastors and church leaders. Jonathan ably shows us how this important letter has much to say to the whole church, even though it is addressed to young Pastor Timothy.

Therefore, our hope and prayer are that this volume – the fifteenth in our *Teaching...* series – will encourage those who bear the joyful yet demanding responsibility of Bible teaching to apply the letter to themselves and to preach and teach it to their churches.

As with other volumes, the introductory section contains basic navigational material to get you into the text of the letter. It covers aspects such as theme, structure and how to plan a series. The 'meat' of the book then works systematically through each major section of the epistle, suggesting preaching and teaching units and including ideas for sermons or questions for Bible studies. These are not there to take the hard work out of preparation but as a starting point to get you thinking about how to teach the material or prepare a Bible study.

As ever, our warm thanks go to the team at Christian Focus for their continued committed partnership in this project. Our prayer continues to be that our speaking Lord would use these volumes to encourage and equip ministers of his word.

David Jackman & Adrian Reynolds
Series Editors
London 2014

Author's Preface

Paul's second letter to Timothy is a rich feast for the gospel minister. It is a letter written from one pastor to another, and it is designed to train, equip and encourage Timothy for the work of ministry. I have counted it a privilege to spend quite a bit of time in 2 Timothy over the last two years, and I am convinced that my teaching and preaching of this letter have done no one more good than me – and I know that the Spirit of God has much yet to do in my heart and life to drive home the powerful lessons of this letter.

I am grateful for the opportunities I have been given to preach and teach this letter – at Christ Church, Westbourne, the PT Cornhill Training Course and Regent College, Vancouver. At each stage and in each context, my grasp of 2 Timothy has been extended and deepened by the comments and questions of those who have listened and responded.

This volume is not an academic study of 2 Timothy. The aim throughout is to make the material accessible and easily navigable. Such a format precludes the opportunity to register each debt I owe to the commentaries I have read and other resources I have used in studying 2 Timothy. The *Further Resources* section at the end of the book will give a clear picture of the range of works I have used, but I would like here simply to acknowledge my very significant debt to the scholars and pastors who have worked hard at the text and have given us such a rich heritage of resources to aid our study of God's word.

Finally, it is a pleasure to record my gratitude to Dick Lucas for his incisive feedback on an earlier draft of this work, to Adrian Reynolds and David Jackman for their invaluable editorial input, and to Celia Reynolds for her kind help in proofreading the manuscript.

Jonathan Griffiths
London, February 2014

How to Use this Book

This guide aims to set out the main logical flow of 2 Timothy in an accessible way with the particular aim of helping the Bible teacher to understand the text and prepare to preach and teach it. This is not a commentary in the conventional sense because there is no pretence that all exegetical possibilities are addressed; very often a position on a point of exegetical contention is adopted and not defended at length.

The book is designed so that the reader can dip into it to consult its treatment of a particular verse or section of 2 Timothy in the *Working through the text* sections without always needing to read the full chapter.[1] However, because the aim is to give the broader logical flow of 2 Timothy and not to provide detailed comment at every point, this guide will serve the reader best if it is used as a base or primary

---

1   As each new verse is addressed for the first time, it is shown in bold (along with its chapter and verse reference) in order to help the reader to be able to refer to the *Working through the text* section as a commentary and to navigate through it more easily.

resource, and if other, more detailed works (for which, see the *Further Resources* section) are consulted in addition to it. If this guide is used mainly as a secondary resource for consultation on individual points of exegesis, it will probably feel inadequate and not serve the reader well.

As is the case across this series of teaching guides, this volume offers suggestions for the theme and aim of each section of 2 Timothy. The 'theme' of the passage is simply an answer to the question, 'What is the message of these verses?', and the 'aim' is an attempt to answer the question, 'What are these verses designed to achieve in the minds, hearts and lives of its hearers?'[2] It is a tremendously valuable exercise to consider those two questions when coming to teach a passage of Scripture. The questions assume that God by his Holy Spirit caused each section of his word to be written in a coherent way (so there will be some unity to its content and message, giving a discernible theme) and for a purpose (so there will be an aim, or series of related aims).

As preachers and teachers of the word who seek to sit under the authority of the word, we will want to ensure that as we teach any given passage, we are saying what it says and seeking to achieve what it seeks to achieve. Thus the theme and aim of the author in this passage should shape the theme and aim of our sermon or Bible study. So, I hope that the suggestions offered here will be a useful starting

---

2   As we will see below, this is an open letter addressed to Timothy but written for the benefit of the whole church. Paul therefore has a dual audience in mind for the letter. Sometimes the aim of a given passage will be quite similar for both Timothy and the church as a whole, but sometimes the purpose of a given passage will be quite different for Timothy and for the rest of the church. For that reason, I will frequently suggest two aims for a given passage: an aim for Timothy (and, by extension, for the pastor-teacher today) and an aim for the wider church.

point for you. I must stress that they are only offered as a starting point. No doubt you will be able to sharpen and improve them as you work at the text.

Similarly the sermon hooks, sermon outlines and Bible study questions offered are given as suggestions and starting points, but are by no means the final word. If anything, these are offered more tentatively than the theme and aim suggestions. Different outlines and different study questions will be appropriate in different contexts. You are welcome to use the material here as you see fit, but my expectation is that each reader will need to develop any suggestions here for their local context.

Part 1:
Introductory Material

I

Getting our Bearings in 2 Timothy

'Everything I know I learned from five wise men, "Who, What, Where, Why and When."' The ditty may be familiar, but its usefulness should not be underestimated. These five 'wise men' are great friends to the Bible teacher when it comes to tackling a new Bible book.[1] We will begin by asking those five questions of 2 Timothy (although for convenience we will change the order).

Who?

Paul

Paul writes 2 Timothy with the authority of an apostle (1:1), the urgency of one who believes that the gospel is a matter of life and death (1:1, 10-11), and the loving concern of a spiritual father (1:2-4).[2] It is almost certainly

---

1   I am grateful to David Cook both for the ditty and for the helpful model of approaching a fresh Bible book with these five simple questions. The idea originally comes from Rudyard Kipling's *Just So Stories*.

2   The question of Paul's authorship of 2 Timothy is much disputed. We will assume the authenticity of his authorship here and discuss the issue in more detail below.

Paul's final letter. He has been abandoned by his friends (1:15, 4:9-16) and is languishing in prison (1:8, 1:16), expecting an imminent death: 'For I am already being poured out like a drink offering, and the time has come for my departure.' (4:6). Paul knows that he stands at the close of the apostolic era, and he is acutely aware that, humanly speaking, the future of gospel ministry now lies in the hands of young leaders like Timothy. He writes 2 Timothy to set for Timothy (and, by extension, for us) the authoritative pattern and agenda for gospel ministry in the post-apostolic era.

Timothy

Timothy, whom Paul describes as his 'dear son' (1:1) in the faith, has been his missionary companion for over fifteen years (as indicated by the chronology of Paul's ministry drawn from Acts). His mother and grandmother (but apparently not his father) were believers (Acts 16:1, 2 Tim. 1:5). He joined Paul's missionary team at Lystra (Acts 16:1-3) and went on to collaborate with Paul on several letters (1 and 2 Thessalonians, 2 Corinthians, Philippians, Colossians and Philemon). Paul placed him in charge of the church at Ephesus (1 Tim. 1:3), where it seems he remains at the time of writing 2 Timothy.

Timothy is a younger minister as Paul writes his two letters to him. That much is clear from the fact that Paul needs to exhort him not to allow others to look down on him because of his youth (1 Tim. 4:12) and from his concern that Timothy will be subject to 'the evil desires of youth' (2 Tim. 2:22). Some have taken the view that the tone of Paul's correspondence with Timothy indicates not only that he was young, but also that he was something of a weakling, meriting the nickname 'Timid Timothy'. Representative of this view is Stott's description of Timothy as 'young in years, frail in physique, retiring in disposition.'[3]

Certainly Paul does speak of Timothy's 'frequent illnesses' (1 Tim. 5:23), but we must be careful not to place Timothy in a special 'weakling' bracket and so dismiss Paul's instructions to him as applying specifically to the unusually weak. After all, 'what minister under pressure hasn't felt that pressure in his stomach'!'[4] Paul's exhortation to Timothy to set aside timidity (1:7) and to be unashamed of the gospel (1:8) does not indicate that Timothy was especially cowardly; it simply reflects the fact that living for Jesus and proclaiming Jesus will put Timothy under fire. All gospel ministers need to heed the call to boldness and steadfastness because all gospel ministers will be tempted to shrink back under pressure. So Paul's instructions to Timothy are not confined in their relevance to the young or the feeble, but they have implications for all who would live for Jesus and make him known.

The church

The church at Ephesus that is currently under Timothy's care is threatened by the presence of false teachers in its midst. Men like Hymenaeus and Philetus (2:17-18) have already disturbed the faith of members of the church family, and Paul expects more of the same to come (3:6-9). Paul addresses his letter to Timothy, but he intends for this to be an open letter, read aloud to the congregation. This would fit with what we know of the reception of other New

---

3   Stott, J.W., *The Message of 2 Timothy* (Nottingham, UK: Inter-Varsity Press, 1998), p. 20.

4   Lucas, R.C., Address on 2 Timothy given at The Proclamation Trust Evangelical Ministry Assembly 1986. An audio recording is available online at www.proctrust.org.uk.

Testament letters and is indicated by Paul's use of the plural pronoun at the close of the letter: 'The Lord be with your spirit. Grace be with you [plural].' The letter is addressed to Timothy, but it is *for* the whole church at Ephesus.

The false teachers

As with Paul's other letters, it is important for us to take note of the opponents (current and potential) he has in view here, because understanding what we can of the threats he perceives will sharpen our understanding of his response and help us to apply his teaching more precisely. That having been said, we need to exercise due humility and caution because our information is limited. Scholars can easily get carried away when speculating about the opponents that stand in the background in Paul's letters. To take one striking example, scholars have made 44 separate possible identifications of the opponents in Colossae,[5] while one prominent NT scholar questions whether there were any opponents at all.[6] In the case of the Pastoral Epistles, scholars have proposed at least 19 different identifications of the opponents in view.[7] So, we need to tread carefully and ensure that we do not go beyond the evidence.

We are, however, told *something* about the opponents Paul has in view, and what we are told is quite illuminating. The first opponents we meet are Hymenaeus and Philetus

---

5   According to Gunther's analysis in Gunther, J.J., *St Paul's Opponents and Their Backgrounds: A Study of Apocalyptic and Jewish Sectarian Teachings* (Leiden, Netherlands: Brill, 1973), pp. 3-4.

6   Hooker, Morna D., *From Adam to Christ: Essays on Paul* (Cambridge: Cambridge University Press, 1990), pp. 121-138. I became aware of both Gunther's and Hooker's observations through Schreiner's comments in Schreiner, Thomas R., *Interpreting the Pauline Epistles, 2nd Edition* (Grand Rapids: Baker Academic, 2011), p. 32.

7   Gunther, *Opponents*, pp. 4-5.

'who have wandered away from the truth. They say that the resurrection has already taken place, and they destroy the faith of some' (2:18). These men evidently started on the side of orthodox truth, but have since 'wandered away' (aren't these so often the most dangerous opponents – I am always wary when I see a book written by a 'former evangelical'). Their brand of heresy is the message that the resurrection has already happened. That is, they are denying the future bodily resurrection of believers and are insisting instead that the resurrection is an exclusively spiritual reality which is already the possession of God's people. According to their heresy, God's people are even now living in the resurrection age. All the blessings of that age are here now to enjoy in their fullness.

Unsurprisingly, such a message destroys the faith of some (2:18). It destroys faith because it leads to massive disappointment. For those who believe that they are experiencing the fullness of the blessings of salvation now, the sufferings and disappointments of life are magnified to faith-nullifying proportions. After all, if this life is as good as it gets, it would hardly be worth being a Christian. And if the victorious resurrection age has room for a suffering and imprisoned apostle like Paul, that makes for a particular disappointment. Surely God's people – and the leaders of God's people especially – should be living the good life. Presumably this heresy in Ephesus is one reason why Paul is so concerned to tell Timothy and the church there that they need to be ready to suffer (3:12).

Perhaps a bit further off into the horizon, Paul sees other false teachers threatening the church. They are among the ungodly people who will appear during the final stage of salvation history (that is, this present age) who will be characterised by love of self, money and pleasure, but who do not love all that is good or God himself (3:1-5). Among these people there will be those who oppose the truth and derail the unstable and impressionable within the church family. These false teachers may have a 'form of godliness' (there will be some superficial plausibility about them, 3:5) but ultimately they are not on the side of the truth and they are rejected by God (3:8).

Like Demas – who deserted Paul – these false teachers have a disease of the heart whereby their love is misdirected away from God, its rightful object, and is instead directed toward this present world (4:9; see, by contrast, 4:8). In a sense there is an overlap between the false teachers of 3:6-9 and the false teachers of 2:18: both are interested in what this world can offer them here and now, and they have lost sight of their future hope. To combat both groups of false teachers and their twisted theology, Paul affirms the reality and rightness of his present suffering for the gospel and the call for Timothy and others to follow in his steps.

Where?

Paul writes 2 Timothy from Rome (1:17), the heart of the Empire, where he is in chains (1:8, 16) awaiting his death (4:6). We have little reason to doubt that Timothy is still in Ephesus (1 Tim. 1:3), where he has been providing leadership to the church.

Ephesus was a great city in every respect. In terms of its political significance, it was capital of the Roman province of Asia and (at an estimated 250,000 people) one of the largest cities of the Roman Empire. Its location made it centrally important for trade in the region; it sat at the eastern tip of the Mediterranean where Asia meets Europe, at the end of the Asiatic caravan route, and it had a large natural harbour (which is now silted in). As far as culture was concerned, the city boasted a theatre with capacity for over 20,000 people, baths, a great library (built soon after Paul's time), agora[8] and paved roads. It was also a key centre of religion; the city was perhaps most famous for the temple to Artemis (or Diana) that was one of the wonders of the ancient world and that lay a short way outside the (six mile long) city walls.

Paul lived and taught in Ephesus for about 3 years and eventually attracted the attention and the anger of the religious authorities and traders, prompting him to leave (Acts 19). The record of his ministry there in Acts 19 confirms the picture we glean from other sources of a wealthy, cosmopolitan and idolatrous city.

When?

This is almost certainly Paul's final letter. He believes that death is imminent (4:6-7), but he also reckons that there may be a sufficient delay that he will have time to make use of his cloak and scrolls (4:13). Scholars have struggled to fit the journeys mentioned in 1 and 2 Timothy and Titus with those mentioned in Acts. Similarly, the experience of imprisonment reflected here in 2 Timothy does not resonate very well with the kind of prison experience recorded in Acts and the prison epistles (where Paul has a greater degree of freedom and expects to be released). It seems most likely, therefore, that 2 Timothy (along with 1 Timothy and Titus) was written after the close of the

---

8   An agora was an central gathering place in an ancient city; it often served as the focal point of the cultural, political, religious, military and commercial life of the city.

chronology of Acts and reflects a further set of travels and
a second, harsher imprisonment. The Roman historian
Eusebius holds that, after Paul was set free from his first
imprisonment, he continued his ministry of preaching
before being imprisoned in Rome under Nero's reign
(during which time he wrote 2 Timothy) and that he was
martyred during that imprisonment.[9] Nero's persecution
began in A.D. 64 and his reign ended in A.D. 68. If we
accept Eusebius' account (which appears to have much to
commend it), then we have a fairly clear window for the
date of the letter.

Why?

Paul is conscious that he has reached not only the end of
his life but also the end of the apostolic era. In this letter he
is handing on the baton of gospel stewardship and gospel
proclamation to Timothy, who is both his child in the faith
and his trusted protégé. He wants to impress upon Timothy
(and the wider church as it listens in) what is really essential
when it comes to guarding the gospel and making it known.
As he looks far into the horizon of the post-apostolic future,
he sets out in 2 Timothy his key priorities for the church in
this new era. The urgency of doing so is heightened by the
presence of opposition in Ephesus.

What?

What kind of document is 2 Timothy? It is both a genuine
letter from a spiritual father and apostle to his spiritual
child and successor, and it is an open letter for the church,
intended to be heard by the whole church family (and

---

9   *Historia Ecclesiastica* 2.22.2, 7.

possibly intended to be preserved and circulated more widely).[10]

What does the letter say? As suggested earlier, when approaching any Bible book it is always a helpful exercise to ask what the book is basically about (the 'theme') and what the author was trying to achieve in writing it (the 'aim'). In the case of 2 Timothy, we may summarise the theme as follows: *The pastor-teacher must guard and proclaim the apostolic gospel despite opposition, following Paul's example.* For Timothy (and other pastor-teachers who read this letter), the aim is: *Guard the gospel through faithful proclamation; endure the suffering that will result.* It is important to remember that Paul has two primary recipients in view for his letter: Timothy and the church family at Ephesus. That second group points us to a secondary aim for the letter: *Seek and prayerfully support faithful ministry.*

A further note on the authorship of 2 Timothy

Paul's authorship of 2 Timothy and the other Pastoral Epistles was almost universally accepted until the mid-19th century, but since then rejection of Pauline authorship has become widespread and, in some quarters, the standard view. Our initial instinct may be to ask whether this question, to which most commentaries give detailed attention, is actually very important. Before addressing the issue briefly, I would like to suggest three reasons why it is important for the Bible teacher to give at least some consideration to it:

---

10   Presumably Paul would have known that his earlier letters were being kept and used more widely, and so he may well have written 2 Timothy with that expectation in mind.

+ The subject comes up in all the major commentaries on the Pastoral Epistles. If we do not give time and attention to forming a reasoned view and conviction about the issue of authorship of these biblical texts, we will endlessly find ourselves spending time going round the issue on each occasion that we return to the Pastorals and engage with the commentaries. It is worth the investment of some time and mental energy to settle the issue.

+ The Pastoral Epistles are vital documents because they show us what faithful gospel ministry looks like. However, the authorship debate has served to marginalise them in the life of the church. Try as we may to smooth over the issue, the simple fact is that if 2 Timothy was not written by the Apostle Paul (despite claiming to be so), we will take it less seriously, and its authority and impact within the church will be undermined.

+ With any Bible book, part of the teaching exercise is to see how the book applied to its first readers (or hearers) in its original historical context. We need to figure that out before we can seek to apply the message of the book to our own context. If the real original context of 2 Timothy is not the imprisoned Apostle Paul writing from prison to Timothy in Ephesus in the mid-sixties of the first century, but rather some anonymous figure writing to a quite different recipient in, say, the mid-second century, then the job of discerning the meaning of the letter for the first recipients in the original context is well nigh impossible. And consequently we are greatly hindered in our ability to teach and preach the book effectively today.[11]

Those who maintain that another writer wrote 2 Timothy (and the other Pastoral Epistles) under Paul's name generally point to the following considerations to support their view:[12]

1) **Historical.** The visits mentioned in the Pastorals do not seem to fit with the order given in Acts. However, this problem disappears if we assume (as argued above) that after the imprisonment of Acts 28 Paul travelled further and was arrested a second time.

2) **Literary.** The vocabulary of the Pastorals is rather different from the vocabulary of other Pauline letters. However, we must remember that in all his letters Paul is responding to specific situations and concerns, even crises. The letters are occasional literature, not abstract theological treatises. In that light, it stands to reason that much of his vocabulary choices would be driven by the situation addressed, leading naturally to wide variations in vocabulary across his letters. This is particularly clear in the Corinthian correspondence, where scholars

---

11   For this significant point, see Duff, Jeremy, 'A Reconsideration of Pseudepigraphy in Early Christianity,' *Tyndale Bulletin* 50.2 (1999), p. 309.

12   This overview of the arguments in favour of pseudonymous authorship draws on Stott's helpful treatment of the issues and borrows some of his headings. See Stott, *Message*, pp. 14-16. Stott's discussion remains a good introduction to these issues, but for a detailed study it would be necessary to supplement Stott with a further analysis of the practice of pseudonymity in early Christianity and other ancient contexts (for which Mounce is a good starting point; see below).

frequently suggest that Paul is actually quoting in places from letters he has received reporting on the situation in Corinth. More generally, it seems unwise and methodologically suspect to select a particular group of letters and to designate them 'genuinely Pauline', and then to judge the genuineness of other, allegedly more suspect, letters based on their conformity to patterns of style and vocabulary in the accepted letters.

3) **Ecclesiatical.** The pastorals seem to reflect (or, at least, seek to establish) a more developed church structure than we see in, say, Galatians. It is argued that this fact demonstrates that they belong to a later period. However, given that the Pastorals (a) concern the nature of pastoral ministry and (b) are written at the end of the Apostle's ministry with a concern for the life of the church in the post-apostolic era, it should come as no great surprise that they address issues of church leadership, governance and order. Indeed, it would seem strange if they did not.

The practice of pseudonymity. It is argued that writing under a pseudonym was accepted as standard practice both in ancient Judaism and in the early church. While pseudonymous authorship of religious literature was practised and, it seems, accepted at least to some degree within ancient Judaism,[13] the situation was quite different

---

13   Although even here we should exercise caution. With reference to the practice of pseudepigraphy in Jewish apocalyptic literature Donelson concludes that '[i]n no case can it be deduced with certainty that this was done innocently and with no intention to deceive'. Donelson, Lewis R., *Pseudepigraphy and Ethical Arguments in the Pastoral Epistles* (Tübingen, Germany: Mohr Siebeck, 1986), pp. 10-11.

in the early church (as we see below). This fourth argument given in support of pseudonymity should be rejected for the following reasons:[14]

+ There is no evidence of any pseudonymous letter being accepted as authoritative by the early church.[15]

+ There is significant evidence showing that the early church rejected the practice of pseudonymous writing and the authority of pseudonymous letters. The Muratorian Canon (a list of accepted Scripture books going back to 2nd century) records the following regarding the pseudonymous 'Epistle to the Laodiceans' (cf. Col. 4:16): 'There is current also (an epistle) to the Laodiceans, another to the Alexandrians, forged in Paul's name for the sect of Marcion, and several others, which cannot be received into the catholic Church; for it will not do to mix gall with honey'. A letter identified as 'Third Corinthians' was written under Paul's name by a 2nd century bishop who claimed he wrote it out of 'love for Paul'. When he confessed that it was a forgery, he was removed from office due to the recognised seriousness of the offence (see Tertullian, *De Baptismo* 17). Paul himself was aware of at least one pseudepigraphal letter in circulation bearing his name

---

14   The following overview of the issues draws especially on Mounce's informative and judicious discussion (although the main points raised here and the ancient sources referenced feature in a number of treatments of this issue in the secondary literature); quotations from original sources are from Mounce, W.D., *Pastoral Epistles, Word Biblical Commentary* Vol. 46 (Nashville, USA: Thomas Nelson, 2000), p. cxxiv-cxxv.

15   See also Donelson, *Pseudepigraphy*, p .11; Marshall, I.H., *The Pastoral Epistles, International Critical Commentary* (London, U.K.: T&T Clark International, 1999), p. 82.

and was concerned that the church should not accept or believe such a document (2 Thess. 2:2). He took the step of developing his own trademark to demonstrate the authenticity of his own letters (2 Thess. 3:17, 1 Cor. 16:21, Gal. 6:11, Col. 4:18, Philem. 19).

+   The moral issue. Many argue that the practice of writing under an assumed name was so widely accepted in the ancient world that there was no moral concern surrounding it.[16] Marshall rightly notes, however, that '[t]he weakness of this argument is that it measures the morality of pseudonymity by the standards of the non-Christian world rather than by the standards of Christian teaching.'[17] Not only is 2 Timothy written under Paul's name, but purports to rest on and reflect a network of personal relationships and a history of personal interactions. Particularly striking are Paul's references to his affection for Timothy and his longing to see him again (2 Tim. 1:2-4; 4:9, 21). If none of that is genuine, it really amounts to a large-scale deception. In light of such deception, it would be very hard to accept the teaching and the exhortations of the author.

+   In addition to these general considerations, there is also the significant observation that '[t]here are no known explicit statements from the first several centuries of the Christian church to the effect that someone knew

---

16   This widely accepted assumption is itself open to question. Even in the secular world, when documents that claimed 'prescriptive and proscriptive authority' were found to be written under an assumed name, they were no longer accepted. Donelson, *Pseudepigraphy*, p. 11.

17   Marshall, *The Pastoral Epistles*, p. 82.

the Pastoral Epistles were pseudonymous....'[18] Surely, had it been known and accepted that these were documents written under a pseudonym, we might find some hint of recognition of that fact in the early church – but there is none.

So, then, we have a genuine letter of Paul addressed to Timothy, but also designed to be read out to the church at Ephesus. This is Paul's final letter, written from prison in Rome, during his second, harsher imprisonment, which almost certainly occurred during Nero's persecution. He wrote the letter in order to combat false teaching and to issue a charge to Timothy; namely, that he should guard the apostolic gospel through proclaiming it and be willing to endure the suffering that he will encounter as he does so. It defines for church leaders and for all believers the authoritative pattern of gospel ministry in the post-apostolic age.

---

18   Porter, Stanley E., 'Pauline Authorship and the Pastoral Epistles: Implications for Canon', *Bulletin for Biblical Research* 5 (1995), p. 115.

2

WHY SHOULD WE PREACH AND
TEACH 2 TIMOTHY?

We can feel somewhat reluctant to preach and teach the Pastoral Epistles today because of some of the controversial and hard-hitting things that they say (particularly surrounding the roles of men and women in the family and the church). Although 2 Timothy is perhaps less controversial in this respect than 1 Timothy or Titus, it can nonetheless be easily swept aside with them for the same reason. Added to the fear of controversy is the question of relevance: the Pastorals address pastors in the first instance, and we preachers wonder if we can apply these letters relevantly and engagingly to a whole church family.

However, Paul, for his part, was convinced that the whole congregation needed to hear what he had to say to Timothy about gospel stewardship, gospel living and gospel ministry. We can be in no doubt that we and our churches need to hear every word of Paul's message in our day. Needless to say, it is a dangerous thing to marginalise and ignore any part of God's word, and this is certainly the case with 2 Timothy. The following are a few reasons, among others, why we need to preach and teach 2 Timothy and why it will do us and our churches much good if we do so:

1) Along with the other Pastoral Epistles, 2 Timothy sets out for us the authoritative pattern for gospel ministry in the post-apostolic age. Often ministers and congregations are confused about what gospel ministry should look like – where time and money should be spent, what the job description of the church ministry staff should contain, what should shape the broader priorities of the church as a whole body. Second Timothy teaches us how to establish right priorities. If we want to get these right ourselves as leaders, and if we want our church family to support us, we need to make it our business to know 2 Timothy.

2) It calls us afresh to acknowledge the apostolic authority of Paul and his message, and to maintain loyalty to his writings. So often throughout the letter Paul reminds Timothy of his own personal example and of the message that he has proclaimed ('You, however, know all about *my* teaching, *my* way of life, *my* purpose....' 2 Tim 3:10, italics mine). Timothy is to hand on the things that he has 'heard *me* say' (2:2, italics mine). Being ashamed of Paul is closely linked to being ashamed of Jesus (see 1:8). We today need to be reminded of the authority of the apostle and his message because some of the strongest opposition convinced evangelicals encounter – both within the church and in society at large – is directed precisely against Paul and his teaching. We need to remember that the gospel we

proclaim is none other than the apostolic gospel, and we need to be mindful that if we were to set the apostle Paul and his teaching aside, we would reject none other than Jesus himself.

3) It shows us how to seek to raise up leaders for the future. In 2 Timothy we see Paul at work discipling, training and mentoring a key leader for the future, and we see him thinking aloud about the shape of his broader ministry team. If we want to serve the cause of the gospel beyond our geographical patch and beyond the time of our own ministry, we need to learn, under God, to raise up leaders for the future. Second Timothy shows us how to do that.

4) It commends to us a godly pattern of life for the gospel minister and rebukes us in our ungodliness. This, obviously, will do much good to the church's leaders. It will also show congregations how to pray for the leadership. And it will show all the members of the church family who exercise some form of Bible teaching ministry how to go about their ministry in a godly way.

5) It teaches us how to handle doctrinal conflict. Conflict over the truth will be a feature of the life of any minister and any church. Paul shows us how to respond to different kinds of conflict with discernment and godliness.

6) It reminds us why the gospel (and gospel ministry) matters. Paul has a consistently eternal perspective throughout the letter, and he casts all his teaching about ministry in the light of eternity. How we and

our church families need to be reminded that the gospel really is a matter of life and death!

7) It sets realistic expectations about life and ministry for God's people in this age. We naturally long for a life of ease and comfort. We readily convince ourselves that Jesus' job is to make life easier and more pleasant for us. But Paul reminds us that life as a follower of Jesus in this age will mean suffering now and glory later. This will be especially true for the gospel minister.

8) It teaches a church family what to pray for. Many of the lessons and applications of the letter will be directed in the first instance to the pastor-teacher. Often the applications for the church family will be secondary – and frequently the natural application will be for the church family to pray that the leaders of the church will be enabled to do what Paul has instructed them to do. So, for the regular church member, 2 Timothy is a something of a guidebook on how to pray for their leaders.

9) It establishes the priority of the preaching of God's word. The climax of 2 Timothy is 4:1-2 and the charge for Timothy to preach the word. In light of all the dangers, opposition and false teaching Timothy will face, and in light of the eternal stakes of the gospel, the central thing Timothy is to do is preach the word. How desperately we need to establish and maintain that priority in our churches. Ministers need to be reminded of it and churches need to have that priority written into their very DNA.

Applying the book of 2 Timothy today

Paul's second letter to Timothy is not an immediately straightforward book to preach and apply to a whole church family. It is written by one pastor-teacher to another, and it concerns primarily the business of gospel ministry. In one sense, the most natural context for teaching 2 Timothy is to teach it to a group of modern-day 'Timothies', that is, to a group of people who are set apart for full-time Bible teaching ministry. In that rarefied kind of a context (perhaps a retreat for ministers), it would be possible to make fairly direct applications from 2 Timothy throughout a teaching series. But in a normal church context, very often the applications from 2 Timothy will be somewhat secondary or derived applications. It will not do to pretend that everyone in the congregation is more or less in Timothy's position and so to apply every lesson from the whole letter directly to everyone listening. This is the easy (if not the most accurate) way to preach 2 Timothy, not least because it will tend to make our preaching feel more immediately relevant to individuals within the congregation. We will feel a constant pull to handle 2 Timothy in this way, but we who teach and preach the letter need to be careful not to fall into the rut of doing this.

That having been said, we must avoid the opposite danger of believing that 2 Timothy has really very little to say to a whole church family. Remember that it was written as an 'open letter', addressed *to* Timothy, but designed *for* the whole church family to hear (note again the plural 'you' in 4:22). With that in mind, it would be useful to bear the following general lines of application in mind throughout a teaching series on the letter:

+ Second Timothy shows us what kind of ministry we should seek to sit under. Churches need to be taught and prepared for appointing new ministers and new members of a ministry team. Churches with elected eldership structures need to know what pressures their elders will face and what kind of people they would like to lead them before they set about choosing them. Members of the church family will inevitably move on from time to time, and they need to have a biblically-shaped view of what healthy ministry looks like as they look for a new church.

+ Second Timothy will help a church family to submit to and follow godly leadership as they see the God-given patterns and priorities of 2 Timothy being implemented by their leaders.

+ Second Timothy teaches a church family how to pray for its leaders. It shows the church family the pressures their ministers will face and the priorities they need to maintain.

+ Many churches will have a number of pastor-teachers in the church family, so it is likely that there will be a number of 'Timothies' sitting under the teaching and preaching of the letter. The lessons about gospel ministry and the pastor-teacher will, of course, apply directly to them.

+ In a derived and secondary sense, the lessons of 2 Timothy about the priorities and pressures of ministry will apply to all those in the church family who have some form of Bible teaching ministry (home group leadership, Sunday school teaching, one-to-one ministry, and so on). This will be a very significant line of application, but it needs to be handled in a nuanced and thoughtful way throughout.

Because the applications that the preacher will draw from 2 Timothy will vary from setting to setting – and will be potentially quite diverse even within a single setting – it will probably be most helpful to construct sermon outlines and headings that are shaped by the theological lessons of a passage, rather than its direct lines of application. Often it can make for more engaging preaching to have sermon points and headings that are framed as direct applications of the truth of a passage, but that will generally not be easy to achieve for 2 Timothy (unless the preacher can be confident that a single line of application will apply to the whole congregation). Often the lines of application for different groups of hearers within a given congregation will be quite diverse. Usually, then, it will be easier to state truths in sermon headings and then apply each truth specifically to different groups within that point (pastor-teachers, praying church members, church members with specific word ministry responsibilities, etc.).

3

IDEAS FOR PREACHING OR TEACHING
A SERIES ON 2 TIMOTHY

If you were preaching or teaching 2 Timothy in the highly
unusual context of a conference for ministers where the
application of the letter would be direct at every stage, there
would be scope for, and merit in, exploring all the nooks
and crannies of the letter. Given that applying 2 Timothy
to a whole church family is a somewhat indirect exercise,
I would suggest that any series on 2 Timothy should
be kept from dragging on too long, for fear of wearying
both congregation and preacher (this comment is by no
means intended to undermine the value and importance
of preaching 2 Timothy; we simply need to be realistic
about what people are able to digest and what will be most
edifying for a church family). With that in mind, I will not
suggest an outline for a particularly slow-paced series on
2 Timothy.

Below are two proposals; one for a fast-paced series on
the book (which would function as an overview rather than
a detailed exposition), and one for a medium-paced series

(which would allow for close attention to the text without getting bogged down).

A fast-paced (overview) series

(1) Faithful gospel stewardship (ch. 1)

(2) Costly gospel service (ch. 2)

(3) Standing apart for the gospel (ch. 3)

(4) Gospel proclamation and gospel strategy (ch. 4)

A medium-paced series

(1) A precious gospel heritage (1:1-7)

(2) Unashamed gospel stewardship (1:8-18)

(3) The suffering gospel servant (2:1-13)

(4) The unashamed gospel workman (2:14-26)

(5) Terrible times and terrible people (3:1-9)

(6) Keeping your balance in terrible times (3:10-17)

(7) Preach the word (4:1-5)

(8) A pattern of faithfulness (4:6-8)

(9) The faithful gospel strategist (4:9-22)

In this guide we will follow this second, more detailed, outline.

A note on preaching single verses

Second Timothy contains a number of well-known individual verses which we may want to preach or teach on their own or include within a topical series on, for example, the theology of ministry or the theology of the word of God. The main thing to remember when doing this is to set these individual verses within their context in the book and to ensure that our teaching from these individual verses resonates appropriately with Paul's broader purpose and concern in the letter.

There are one or two verses that we will almost certainly teach wrongly if we do not pay adequate attention to the context. Perhaps most vulnerable to misuse is 2 Timothy 2:22, which has been pressed into service on countless occasions to teach young people about the importance of sexual purity. But even a cursory glance at its context confirms that this is not what Paul had in mind. The broader context shows that the issue at hand is the handling of conflict with false teachers and opponents, and the 'evil desires of youth' are the tendencies of young people to delight in arguing. Another verse that is often taken out of its context is 2 Timothy 3:16, which is primarily intended to impress upon Timothy the sufficiency of Scripture for his ministry (and so to encourage him to keep using it as the basis of all his ministry, unlike the false teachers). However, plucked from context, the issue of Scripture's sufficiency is often forgotten when teaching 3:16, and it is used to teach the related doctrine of Scriptural authority. So, by all means preach individual verses and use individual verses to teach doctrine as part of larger overviews of doctrinal themes within Scripture – but be sure to take proper account of the immediate context and the broader theme and aim of 2 Timothy.

Part 2
PREACHING OR TEACHING A SERIES ON 2 TIMOTHY

I

A PRECIOUS GOSPEL HERITAGE
(1:1-7)

Paul, an apostle of Christ Jesus by the will of God, according to the promise of life that is in Christ Jesus,

To Timothy, my dear son:

Grace, mercy and peace from God the Father and Christ Jesus our Lord.

I thank God, whom I serve, as my forefathers did, with a clear conscience, as night and day I remember you in my prayers. Recalling your tears, I long to see you, so that I may be filled with joy. I have been reminded of your sincere faith, which first lived in your grandmother Lois and in your mother Eunice and, I am persuaded, now lives in you also. For this reason I remind you to fan into flame the gift of God, which is in you through the laying on of my hands. For God did not give us a spirit of timidity, but a spirit of power, of love and of self-discipline.

Introduction

In one sense these verses feel like a somewhat formulaic and predictable preface to the main body of a Pauline letter – as though Paul were just warming up before he really got going. But we must be careful to slow down and hear what Paul is really saying in these verses and to understand what he is really doing. P.T. O'Brien demonstrated some time ago that Paul's prayers and prayer reports at the opening of his letters often take us to the very heart of his concerns in a given letter, and that is certainly the case here.[1] Remember that Paul is preparing to outline for Timothy his responsibilities as a gospel steward and church leader as he prepares to hand over the baton at the end of his own ministry. Here in these opening verses Paul reminds Timothy of his own apostolic authority and of their bond together (both of which are crucial to the handover that Paul is preparing for), and then he reminds Timothy of the resources that God has given him which will equip him for the momentous task that lies ahead.

Listening to the text

Context and structure

The opening verses of the letter reflect Paul's typical pattern of using a Christianised modification and expansion of a standard Graeco-Roman letter style: a personal introduction (v. 1), followed by an address and blessing (v. 2). Next follows a report of Paul's prayer of thanksgiving for Timothy (vv. 3-5). The section ends with an instruction for Timothy that flows from Paul's prayer for him (v. 7).

---

1   O'Brien, P.T., *Introductory Thanksgivings in the Letters of Paul* (Leiden, Netherlands: Brill, 1977), passim, but especially pp. 261-263.

Further instructions and exhortations for Timothy will flow from this prayer report in the section that follows (and, indeed, through the letter as a whole).

Working through the text

As is his habit, Paul introduces himself as **'an apostle of Christ Jesus'** (1:1). The fact that he has been set apart by Jesus and **'by the will of God'** gives him the authority to teach and exhort Timothy as he will do throughout the letter. It is a reminder to Timothy and to the church family listening in that they must heed what Paul has to say. More than that, Paul's apostleship is **'according to the promise of life that is in Christ Jesus'**. That is, Paul's apostleship is grounded in, and concerned with, the gospel of life. These are poignant words coming from a man who expects to die soon (4:6) and who will call Timothy and all believers to face with boldness the harsh reality of persecution (3:12). For the believer, dying with Christ comes before living with him (2:11), but the promise of life is assured. This life is the theme of Paul's message and ministry. Whatever hard realities must be confronted in 2 Timothy, they are confronted within the context of a clear awareness and assurance of the life that Jesus has secured for his people through his death and resurrection.

Paul counts Timothy his **'dear son'** in the faith (1:2). It may be that this affectionate address reflects the fact that Timothy's conversion was due to Paul's ministry in Lystra (Acts 14:8-20; see Acts 16:1-5). It certainly reflects the fact that Paul had mentored Timothy as a spiritual father (in some sense, taking the spiritual role left vacant by Timothy's own unconverted father; Acts 16:1). Mention of Paul's apostleship (1:1) and Timothy's 'sonship' here are not incidental to Paul's broader concern in the letter. As we have already seen, this letter serves a key function in the process of handing on the baton of Paul's ministry and leadership (although clearly not his actual apostleship) to Timothy, his spiritual child and protégé.

Before issuing any of his instructions or warnings Paul offers first a distinctly Christian greeting and blessing: **'Grace, mercy and peace from God the Father and Christ Jesus our Lord.'** It would be hard to read 2 Timothy without feeling both a rebuke (because the letter inevitably makes us more conscious of our failures in ministry) and a sense of trepidation (because it speaks plainly about the challenges ahead). It is therefore no mistake that Paul leads the letter with a reminder of God's wonderful 'grace', which encompasses his redemption of his people through the work of Christ and his sustaining them through the power of his Holy Spirit. Like Timothy, we contemporary readers of this letter need to be grounded in the redeeming and sustaining grace of God if we are to face the challenges of the letter without feeling condemned for past failures or daunted by what the future may hold. God's grace is tied to his 'mercy' toward sinners (that is, his refraining from pouring upon us the judgment we deserve) and issues in 'peace'. This peace comprises peace between us and God (where once there was hostility), peace between us and other believers, and then a peaceful outlook on a stormy future, knowing that all is ultimately well because all has been made right between the believer and the sovereign God.

In Paul's prayer (or report of his prayers; **1:3-5**) he is doing at least two things concurrently: (1) he is pouring out genuine thanksgiving to God for the way he has prepared Timothy for the ministry he now has and for the challenges that lie ahead (both of which will feature centrally in the letter); and (2) he is providing a model from his own ministry of personal discipleship and mentorship as he reveals his heart and his prayer life, in order that Timothy might learn and appropriate his model (see 2:2, where some implications of Paul's model of ministry become particularly clear for Timothy). As noted already, Paul's prayers at the opening of his letters are no mere window-dressing, but rather they take us to the very heart of his priorities and concerns for the rest of the letter. This is certainly the case for 2 Timothy.

In terms of thanksgiving, Paul is grateful for Timothy's **'sincere faith'**. That is, he sees the mark of true and persevering faith in Timothy. There are plenty of impostors and disingenuous believers around Ephesus and in Paul's broader acquaintance (1:15, 2:17, 4:10; see also 3:1-9), so Paul is deeply grateful to the Father for raising up and keeping Timothy. Paul notes with gratitude that Timothy's faith lived first in his **'grandmother Lois'** and **'mother Eunice'**. As was the case for Paul himself (1:3), Timothy had the great privilege of being taught the knowledge of God from infancy. Paul is thankful for Timothy's sincere faith and his heritage of faith because this grounding in the truth will provide the ballast he needs to withstand what lies ahead as he takes hold of the baton of ministry and leadership from Paul. In this grateful acknowledgment of the importance of Timothy's heritage of faith, we catch a glimmer of the tremendous worth of Christian family. Before ever Timothy became a Christian believer or a Christian leader, in the background were Lois and Eunice praying for him and teaching him God's word. Paul knows the fruit, under God, of their ministry, and he is filled with thanksgiving.

Paul's secondary aim here is to show Timothy something of the inner workings of his heart and his prayer life as a Christian leader in order that Timothy might be able to follow in his steps.[2] Time and time again in this letter Paul will tell Timothy what he needs to do and then will show him how he himself has lived out the principles he commends. Throughout the letter Paul is self-consciously recording his personal example that Timothy might follow it. Two features stand out here. First, we see Paul's genuine affection for Timothy. He is his 'dear son' and he **'long[s] to see [him], that [he] may be filled with joy'** (1:4). Paul really loves Timothy. His affection for this younger minister goes beyond bare professional interest. For a mentoring and discipling relationship to bear lasting fruit it must be sincere and deep-rooted in this way. Second, Paul is committed to praying for Timothy. His prayers for Timothy are not occasional and haphazard as so many of our prayers are; no, **'night and day I constantly remember you in my prayers'** (1:3). He is committed to daily and persevering prayer for Timothy, and it is quite clear that he laid the particular concerns of this letter before the Lord in prayer before he put pen to paper. Here is a model for Timothy and for us.

Paul now moves on to his first instruction, an instruction that flows directly from his thanksgiving: **'For this reason I remind you to fan into flame the gift of God'** (1:6). Because Timothy is Paul's spiritual 'son', a true believer with a great heritage of faith, he must take seriously the job before him and make good use of the gift he has been given.

---

2   It is striking, but not surprising, that Paul sets his faithful service of God in a line of continuity with that of his 'forefathers' (1:3), thereby affirming that his Jewish ancestors who served God faithfully before the arrival of Christ did so as genuine believers and true servants of God.

The nature of the gift is not specified here, but we are given insight into that question in 1 Timothy 4, where the gift is also mentioned: 'Until I come, devote yourself to the public reading of Scripture, to preaching and to teaching. Do not neglect your gift, which was given you through a prophetic message when the body of elders laid their hands on you' (1 Tim. 4:13-14). The context of the mention of Timothy's gift there in 1 Timothy 4 indicates strongly that his gift is the gift of preaching and teaching Scripture. This conclusion resonates well with the fact that the central and solemn charge that Paul will give Timothy in his second letter is the charge to 'preach the word' (4:2).

Timothy has been given a gift for word ministry, but the mere presence of the gift does not guarantee its effectiveness. Timothy must 'fan into flame the gift of God'. That is, he must keep working at his preaching and teaching of the word. He must give the time needed to study the Scriptures carefully, to consider the context into which he is preaching and teaching the word, and to develop the right kinds of application for his people. It is possible for a gifted teacher of the word to allow his or her gift to burn down to the point where it is no longer effective, and Timothy must not allow that to happen. Indeed, the fact that Paul needs to remind and exhort Timothy to fan the gift into flame shows us that the natural tendency of the gifts of word ministry will be to burn down and dwindle unless they are carefully cultivated and regularly rekindled.

Paul speaks of this gift as being in Timothy '**through the laying on of my hands**'. Again, the reference to Timothy's gift in 1 Timothy 4:14 sheds some light on what may be meant here. Assuming that both passages refer to the same gift and same event (which seems most likely), Paul then was one of the elders who laid hands on Timothy. So in 2 Timothy 1, where the relationship between Paul and Timothy is so much in view, Paul happily refers to the time when he personally laid hands on Timothy without mentioning the other elders who also participated in Timothy's 'ordination'. The fact that in 1 Timothy the gift came through a 'prophetic message' indicates that the gift was God-given, not imparted by the elders. They responded to the prophetic message of God (however given; see also 1 Tim. 1:18) that Timothy was gifted by him and was to be set apart for word ministry. That gift – whether given previously or at the time of Timothy's setting apart – in any case became active when he was set apart by the elders for the ministry of the word. Paul refers to that event in shorthand here in 2 Timothy 1:6, but it would not be right to take from this condensed reference the implication that the gift for word ministry is imparted by people rather than by God.

Following on from the exhortation to fan into flame the gift of God comes the reminder that God himself has supplied the resources necessary for this work in the gift of his Spirit. Rather than shrink back from the bold proclamation of the word, Timothy is to proclaim it with all energy and forthrightness because the Holy Spirit is not a Spirit of timidity. It would be possible to take reference here to 'a spirit' as a general reference to an attitude or disposition that God has given to word-ministers ('us') like Paul and Timothy. But the broader context makes an intended reference to the Holy Spirit and his enabling power much more likely.[3] In the following verse the call to suffer for the Gospel 'by the power of God' implies the work of the Spirit, and in verse 14 the power to guard the deposit of the Gospel comes through 'the help of the Holy Spirit who lives in us'.

---

3   Neither the 1984 NIV nor the ESV capitalise the word 'spirit' in 2 Tim. 1:7. However, the 2011 NIV correctly, in my opinion, renders the word 'Spirit.'

This Holy Spirit who enables word ministry is a 'Spirit of power, of love and of self-discipline'. He gives the power to do the hard work of studying, preaching and teaching the word, week in, week out (and it is hard work!). He gives the word-minister the love for the Saviour and for his people that encourages him to keep going, even when it is hard and seemingly fruitless, and even when opposition comes along (more on that later). And he gives the word-minister the self-control to keep at it, to guard the time needed, and to maintain a godly pattern of life alongside the work.

As is always the case in the Christian life, the dynamic here is of human responsibility and divine enabling operating together. Timothy is called to serve faithfully by fanning into flame his gift. The great comfort is that God, by his sovereign over-ruling in Timothy's life up to this point, and by the power of his Spirit, provides all the resources necessary.

From text to message

Getting the message clear: theme and aim

Theme:	God graciously gives gospel ministers the resources needed for ministry.
Aim (for the pastor-teacher):	Fan into flame the gift of God
Aim (for the church):	Pray for leaders to maintain their gift; prayerfully seek to raise up future leaders.

A way in

In a longer hook designed to function as a general introduction and 'way in' to a new sermon series on 2 Timothy, we might tackle the question of the letter's relevance to the congregation head-on: 'As we begin to study this ancient letter together – a letter written from one pastor to another – we confront immediately the question, "What does it have to do with us?" It would be one thing if we were a group of church leaders studying the letter together; there would be an obvious and immediate relevance. Second Timothy would tell us how to guard and proclaim the gospel in the context of church leadership. For one or two of us here who are in positions of pastoral leadership, that will be directly relevant. But all of us need to be able to recognise and encourage faithful gospel ministry. At some point most of us will move home and need to seek a new church; and some of us may be involved in the process of appointing new ministers to lead the congregation in the future. More immediately, we as a church family need to have a vision for prayerfully encouraging younger people to consider full-time gospel ministry. This opening passage is particularly helpful to us in this. Here in the first seven verses of the letter, Paul gives us a profile of the young Timothy and the influences that have shaped him thus far as a gospel minister and a church leader. And here Paul shows us what it is that equips a young person for church leadership.'

An alternative approach would be to focus more narrowly on these particular verses and the theme of the development of leaders like Timothy: 'When the well-known preacher John Stott died, many Christians wondered where the next leader of his calibre and his stature was to be found. It is an important question – not simply where the next outstanding leader like John Stott will be found, but also where the next generation of ordinary but faithful gospel ministers will come from. Here in these verses from 2 Timothy 1 we are given insight into the making of the Christian leader. This, in turn, will show us how to pray for and encourage the next generation of gospel ministers.'

Ideas for application

+ Ministers of the gospel need grace and the reminder of grace. We never outgrow the gospel, nor do we stop sinning in this life.

+ Authentic ministry rests on prayer. Paul's ministry to Timothy was undergirded by constant prayer, and the concerns of his letter had been prayed through before they had been written. Paul provides a model in this for all gospel ministers.

+ Ministers of the word need to be gifted for their ministry. Timothy needed to fan his gift into flame, but the actual, God-given gift was already there. It would be no good to urge someone who is not gifted for word-ministry just to 'try a bit harder'. If a God-given gift is present in a person, it can be developed and nurtured; but if no gift is there, the person concerned should not consider word-ministry, and should not be encouraged to do so. Being 'nice' and godly is not enough (similarly, being gifted but ungodly will not do!).

+ Those who have been given every spiritual help and gift needed for ministry will still need to work at it. Timothy had everything going for him when it came to word-ministry, but he still needed to be urged to 'fan into flame the gift of God'.

+ The natural tendency of the gifts for word ministry is to diminish and burn out. Just because a Bible teacher was doing well and his gift burned brightly in earlier years, this does not mean that he will continue in the same way automatically and indefinitely. Bible teachers need constantly to 'fan into flame' their gift. That will mean working hard at the text, working hard at application and illustration, listening carefully to feedback and critique. It will mean continuing to put in the long hours in preparation – especially, perhaps, when one has reached the stage when it would be possible to fake it a bit and still sound quite plausible on a Sunday morning!

+ Timothy was privileged both in his believing family and in his discipleship under Paul. These two sets of relationships were crucial in preparing him for ministry. We should prize gospel-centred families and gospel-centred mentoring friendships in the hope that God might use such relationships to raise up Christian leaders like Timothy for future generations. We can so easily under-value the importance of both, but what dividends were reaped under God from the hours that Timothy's grandmother, mother and the Apostle Paul spent praying for Timothy and teaching him the word. What time are we giving to praying for and discipling our children and grandchildren? Are we looking out for younger believers whom we could befriend and encourage in the faith? This last point might be particularly helpful to draw out for older believers and retirees, who may struggle to see where they can serve in the church.

✦ The church family must pray for their minister(s) to fan into flame the gift of God. Those in positions of leadership (elders, church wardens) need to encourage their ministers to do this, perhaps by making more of a priority of study leave for them, or by freeing up time and resources for attending preaching conferences and workshops.

Suggestions for preaching

A possible sermon

It would be entirely possible to preach two or more sermons on these verses, but there are probably very few contexts where it would be helpful to move quite that slowly. I would suggest a two-point sermon along the following lines:

1. The resources of the gospel minister

   a. gospel grace (1:2b)

   b. a gospel mentor (1:3-4)

   c. a gospel family (1:5)

   d. a gospel gift (1:6)

   e. the Spirit of God (1:7)

2. The call of the gospel minister (1:6)

Although each of the sub-points under point 1 would need to be addressed, I would not suggest listing them as sub-points on an outline or presenting them as such verbally (for fear of overloading the congregation with headings); they are simply presented here in a list for clarity. For those in the congregation who exercise some form of word-ministry, point 1 should prompt each one to give thanks for the resources God has given them, and point 2 should act as a challenge. It will be important to flag up the fact that not all gospel ministers will have had the privilege of a gospel family or a gospel mentor; the three essentials for all gospel ministers are, of course, 'gospel grace', 'a gospel gift', and 'the Spirit of God'. For the whole congregation, this sermon should shape priorities for action and prayer in seeking to raise up future Gospel ministers.

Suggestions for teaching

Ensure that any Bible study group has taken the time to read through the whole of 2 Timothy before beginning the first study. If the group has not prepared in this way, it might be possible simply to read out the letter as a group at the start of the first study (it is not too long!).

Questions to help understand the passage

1. In light of the whole letter, why does Paul begin as he does with (a) a reminder of his apostleship; (b) a reminder of the 'promise of life'; and (c) a grace-filled greeting for Timothy (1:1-2)?

2. Why is Paul grateful (1:3-5)?

3. Read 1 Tim. 4:11-14. What do we glean about the nature of Timothy's 'gift' (2 Tim. 1:6)?

4. What is Timothy to do, and how does this relate to the Holy Spirit (1:6-7)?

5. What will a Spirit-filled ministry look like?

Questions to help apply the passage

1. How does this passage teach us to give thanks for, and pray for gospel ministers?

2. How does Paul's example of prayer instruct and challenge us? What practical steps can we take to follow his example?

3. What does this passage teach us about the way that God prepares and raises up ministers? In light of 1:3-5, how can we participate in the work of raising up a new generation of leaders?

4. What will it mean for a Bible teacher to 'fan into flame the gift of God'? If you have a Bible teaching role, what specific steps do you need to take to continue to fan into flame the gift that you have been given?

5. How should we be praying for the Spirit to be at work in the lives of our ministers and in our own lives?

2

UNASHAMED GOSPEL STEWARDSHIP
(1:8-18)

So do not be ashamed to testify about our Lord, or ashamed of me his prisoner. But join with me in suffering for the gospel, by the power of God, who has saved us and called us to a holy life – not because of anything we have done but because of his own purpose and grace. This grace was given us in Christ Jesus before the beginning of time, but it has now been revealed through the appearing of our Saviour, Christ Jesus, who has destroyed death and brought life and immortality to light through the gospel. And of this gospel I was appointed a herald and an apostle and a teacher. That is why I am suffering as I am. Yet I am not ashamed, because I know whom I have believed, and am convinced that he is able to guard what I have entrusted to him for that day.

What you heard from me, keep as the pattern of sound teaching, with faith and love in Christ Jesus. Guard the good deposit that was entrusted to you – guard it with the help of the Holy Spirit who lives in us.

You know that everyone in the province of Asia has deserted me, including Phygelus and Hermogenes.

May the Lord show mercy to the household of Onesiphorus, because he often refreshed me and was not ashamed of my chains. On the contrary, when he was in Rome, he searched hard for me until he found me. May the Lord grant that he will find mercy from the Lord on that day! You know very well in how many ways he helped me in Ephesus.

Introduction

In these verses the theme of suffering, which is never far beneath the surface in 2 Timothy, comes to the fore. This theme and the wonderful reminder of the gospel of life are woven closely together. Paul is only able to suffer because of his gospel hope, and Timothy will only be willing to join him if he remembers it too. Many others have deserted Paul; he is concerned that Timothy should not join them.

Listening to the text

Context and structure

Verse 7 has brought the reminder that the Holy Spirit given to believers is not a Spirit of timidity, but of power, love and self-control. The dual call of verse eight, to be unashamed of the testimony of Jesus (and of Paul) and to share in suffering, is grounded in the reminder of the Spirit's power. This hard call to suffer is followed immediately by a reminder of the gospel (1:9-10), which has brought salvation and the assurance of the defeat of death. In that light, the prospect of suffering for the gospel should not engender overwhelming fear. Paul then turns to his own willingness to face suffering as a minister of the gospel and his concern that Timothy should follow his example by fearlessly guarding the gospel (1:11-14). The section concludes with Paul's disappointing experience of so many who have been unwilling to suffer for the gospel and so have abandoned him (1:15), and with the outstanding example of Onesiphorus, who was willing to bear the cost of standing with Paul (1:16-18). Chapter 2 will continue the call to suffer for the sake of the gospel.

Working through the text

Verse 8, with its call to '**not be ashamed**' but to join '**in suffering for the gospel**', is the central verse of this section. The gift of the Holy Spirit provides the power needed to heed the call to suffer. The gospel itself will provide the motivation (1:9-10). Paul and Onesiphorus will provide positive models of how to join in suffering (1:11-8). The careful stewardship of the gospel for future generations is the purpose of the suffering (1:12-14).

In a context where the gospel is being undermined by spurious false gospels that are outwardly more attractive than the true gospel (and which suggest that suffering is really sub-Christian), Timothy could easily become ashamed of the true gospel.[1] Linked to that, he could easily become ashamed of Paul, the imprisoned apostle of that gospel. As far as Paul is concerned, being ashamed of the gospel of Jesus and being ashamed of him its messenger are two sides of the same coin. Because Paul is 'an apostle of Christ Jesus by the will of God' (1:1) – that is, a duly commissioned authoritative representative of Jesus Christ

---

1 The Greek text literally reads 'do not be ashamed of the testimony of our Lord', meaning either the testimony that Jesus bore (his own teaching of the gospel), or the testimony concerning Jesus that his followers proclaim. The difference between the two options is slight, and the NIV's decision to paraphrase the text as it has does not take us far from its original sense.

– to be ashamed of him is to be ashamed of the gospel of Jesus Christ itself. Rather than be ashamed, Paul calls Timothy to 'join with me in suffering for the gospel'. These, after all, are the only two alternatives. Either Timothy will join in suffering as he stands with Paul and proclaims the true gospel, or he will be ashamed, fall silent, and avoid suffering. He must choose.

Timothy's natural tendency, like ours, will be to choose the easy option. Paul knows this, but he also knows that the believer is given a Spirit, not of timidity, but of power (1:7), so he calls Timothy to this super-human faithfulness 'by the power of God' (1:8). Only by God's power can Timothy choose and then endure suffering for the gospel .

And God is very powerful: he is the one **'who has saved us and called us to a holy life – not because of anything we have done but because of his own purpose and grace'** (1:9). God's work of saving his people rests entirely on his purpose and his power, so this all-powerful God can be relied upon to strengthen Timothy and all his people for unashamed testimony, even under pressure.

Paul will return to the theme of God's great acts of salvation in a moment, but before he does so, he reinforces for Timothy the fact that God has saved him for a purpose, to call us **'to a holy life'** (1:9). This holy life (or, 'holy calling', as it could be rendered more literally) is not a special 'call' to ordained ministry (such use of the language of 'calling' is not found in the New Testament), but, as elsewhere in the New Testament, it is the call of the believer to salvation, to membership of God's people, and then to live a distinctive life, set apart for God's service. For Timothy, that will mean especially accepting the call to be known as belonging to Jesus Christ and associated with his people, and it will require him to be willing to accept the shame and suffering that such association may bring.

To reinforce the reminder of God's great power, and to steel Timothy for any persecution that may come his way, Paul now turns to focus in earnest to the saving work of God in Jesus. The gospel summary that follows is thrilling and full of comfort for any believer, but it is particularly poignant coming from one who expects at any time to die for his faith. The gospel brings great security because it is given to the believer **'in Christ Jesus'** (1:9); that is, the prevenient grace of God joins the believer to Christ and secures him in permanent union with him. That God chose his people for inclusion in Christ before even time began is the very heart of his 'purpose and grace' (1:9). Whatever may come, the believer is safe because he is united to Jesus. God purposed this saving union **'before the beginning of time'** (1:9), which serves as a reminder that the storms of life are temporary and short-lived when viewed from the perspective of God's eternal purposes.

Paul is moving from comfort toward a call to action as he reminds Timothy of the glorious truth that God's eternal purpose **'has been revealed through the appearing of our Saviour, Christ Jesus, who has destroyed death and has brought life and immortality to light through the gospel'** (1:10). God's eternal purpose to bring immortality to his people has come to fulfilment and been made visible through the incarnation ('appearing') and death-destroying death and resurrection of Jesus. The fact that death has been ultimately 'destroyed' does not mean that Jesus' followers will not experience physical death (as the false teachers were evidently claiming, 2:18), but rather that its ultimate and eternal hold has been broken. For the believer, physical death is now simply the entry to life. It is worth pausing and rejoicing in this truth. We so often want to prove to the unbelieving world that the Gospel will make things better for them in this life – and in many ways it will, although it will also bring suffering in this life.[2] But the bigger and more significant truth is that the gospel breaks the power of death and makes things inestimably better for believers in the life to come. And this is a wonderful truth to proclaim to a world that is held in slavery by the fear of death (Heb. 2:15).

This revelation is magnificent news, and so Paul has been appointed to proclaim it as **'a herald and an apostle and a teacher'** (1:11). In passing, note the lines of continuity between Paul's role and that of Timothy. Timothy cannot take over as an apostle; that foundational, doctrine-defining role disappeared with the death of Paul and his fellow-apostles. But Timothy, like Paul, is called to be a 'herald' or 'preacher' (*kērux*); Paul will charge him later in this letter to 'preach (*kēruxon*) the word' (4:2). And Timothy, like Paul, is to be a 'teacher' (*didaskalos*); he is to preach with 'careful instruction' or 'with teaching' (*didachē*, 4:2). Here we see the lines of continuity between Paul's role, Timothy's role and the role of pastor-teachers today. The office of apostleship is closed; the role of preaching and teaching the word continues beyond the apostolic era. Hence Paul's call for Timothy to follow his example.

And now follows the punch-line: **'That is why I am suffering as I am'** (1:12). For such a gospel, and with such security, Paul is willing to suffer in order to proclaim it – and so too should Timothy be willing to suffer. Here is

---

2   See 3:12. Notice again that the false teachers successfully propagated a gospel that was all about the here-and-now, 2:18 (see also 4:10).

one of the many places in 2 Timothy where Paul gives his personal example with the clear intent that Timothy should note and emulate it.[3]

Paul's willingness to suffer unashamedly is not only tied to the security he has in the past work of God; he is also confident concerning God's purposes for the gospel in the future: **'Yet I am not ashamed, because I know whom I have believed, and am convinced that he is able to guard what has been entrusted to me until that day'** (1:12; my revision of NIV translation).[4] To the opponents of the true gospel, Paul's suffering must have seemed futile and pathetic. Surely his message would die with him. But Paul knew better: the God who purposed salvation from the beginning of time, revealed it in the person and work of Jesus, and arranged for its apostolic proclamation would himself guard and keep the gospel until the return of Christ. Paul is fundamentally optimistic as he looks down the ages at the long-term future of gospel ministry.

Paul's optimism does not lead him to complacency, though; it issues forth in instruction for Timothy to **'keep'** Paul's gospel **'as the pattern of sound teaching'** (1:13) and

---

3   Paul presents himself as willing to suffer and unashamed of suffering, and he calls Timothy to join him in that. But we need to see here that the link between gospel ministry and suffering is necessary and intrinsic. Suffering will follow gospel proclamation, whether or not Timothy is prepared for it or willing to face it. Paul's purpose here is not to suggest that Timothy should seek out suffering, but to encourage him to stick with gospel ministry when suffering comes along – which it will.

4   The end of Verse 12b is rendered in the NIV '...to guard what I have entrusted to him for that day'. The Greek could be taken either to refer to the trust that God has given Paul (i.e. the gospel) or the trust that Paul has given God (i.e. his life). The former seems more likely given verse 14 (where the trust is clearly the gospel itself), given Paul's dominant concern throughout the letter with the future guarding and transmission of the gospel, and given how uncharacteristic it would be for Paul to focus in this way on self-concern.

to '**guard the good deposit**' (1:14) of the apostolic gospel. Timothy must be content to be a steward of the gospel and not an innovator (unlike the false teachers so evident in Ephesus). There will be a constant temptation for Timothy, like all teachers of the word, to modify the message in order to have something arresting and headline-catching to say. The false teachers in Ephesus had done precisely that and a number of people had been taken in. But even when faced with the heart-wrenching reality of losing members of the church family to the appealing-sounding message of the false teachers, Timothy must resolve to stick with the apostolic gospel. The gospel that Paul has entrusted to him he is to pass on unchanged to the church and its leaders of the future, even if the result is a ministry that is outwardly less impressive and seemingly less fruitful.

Notice again the dynamic of divine sovereignty and human responsibility operating in tandem here. Paul is convinced that God will guard the gospel; and, being convinced of that, he tells Timothy to get on board with God's agenda and guard the gospel. Along with the instruction for Timothy comes the assurance that God himself will provide all the resources needed for the work of guarding the gospel. Timothy is to keep and guard it '**with faith and love**' that are only found through union with Christ ('**in Christ Jesus**') and '**with the help of the Holy Spirit who lives in us**'.

Paul's concern for Timothy to remain faithful to the apostolic gospel is given added urgency by the fact that '**everyone in the province of Asia has deserted me**' (1:15). Many believers have been unwilling to stand with Paul, unwilling to guard unchanged the apostolic gospel, and unwilling to suffer for the true message.[5] When Paul was imprisoned in Rome and probably in need of friends to provide for his basic needs (prisoners were not necessarily clothed or fed by the state), only Onesiphorus came to his aid (1:16-18). In the deserters from Asia Timothy has an example to shun, and in the bold faithfulness of Onesiphorus he has an example to follow. Paul's confident prayer for Onesiphorus is that he will receive the Lord's saving mercy at the final day. We may presume that Paul would not have had the same confidence for those who deserted him and, by extension, his Lord.

From text to message

Getting the message clear: theme and aim

The heart of this passage is found in the two sets of instructions in verses 8 and 13. They are framed differently, but they share the same concern: namely, that Timothy would stick with proclaiming the true, apostolic gospel, accepting whatever suffering comes with it. Everything else in the passage serves this fundamental aim.

Theme:	Pastor-teachers must be unashamedly faithful to the gospel and to fellow gospel workers.
Aim (for the pastor-teacher):	Do not be ashamed, testify to, and suffer for, the true gospel.

---

5   Paul may have mentioned 'Phygelus and Hermogenes' because they were leaders, but they are otherwise unknown in the NT.

Aim   Pray for leaders to be unashamed
(for the church):   gospel stewards, and join them in
                        suffering.

A way in

One approach would be to focus on the idea of a compelling cause that provides sufficient motivation to suffer. The preacher could open with an example of such a cause (a recent example at the time of writing is the 'Occupy' movement that led people to camp outside in major world cities for weeks on end), and then continue: 'It takes a compelling cause to motivate its proponents to bear significant personal cost. In this passage Paul highlights his experience of suffering, calls Timothy (and us) to join him in suffering – and, crucially, he shows us the cause for which suffering is eminently worthwhile.'

Alternatively, a preacher might focus on the cost itself and ask: 'What do you imagine it will cost you to follow Jesus and to make him known? A bit of money? Some discretionary time at the weekend? A degree of social embarrassment? If that is the extent of our expectation of the cost of following Jesus and serving the gospel, Paul has a wake-up call for us. The call to follow Jesus and to make him known is a call to suffer for him and with his people.'

Ideas for application

+   Where will we be tempted to feel shame at testifying to the true gospel? For many, it will be when facing colleagues, friends, neighbours and family who are opposed to the gospel. For Bible teachers and church leaders, it may be when members of the church are opposed to the gospel, or when other leaders in our denomination teach a distorted gospel. We need to pinpoint the particular pressure points for ourselves and the people in our church or study group. Paul is realistic; refusing to be ashamed will involve accepting the call to suffer (1:8).

+ God provides the power (1:8) to enable us to proclaim unashamedly the true gospel. We need constantly to rely on his strength and ask for his help in this. Remaining faithful is not all about gritting our teeth and getting on with it by ourselves.

+ Delight in the security we enjoy in being part of God's eternal purpose, united with his Son (1:9).

+ God has saved us that we might live a holy life (1:9). We all need to hear this, and gospel ministers need to be reminded that the call to holiness is for us, and not simply for everyone else. A key part of holy living will be remaining faithful to Jesus by unashamedly speaking his truth, even when it makes life difficult to do so.

+ The gospel frees us from the power of death, so we are equipped to face even life-threatening opposition if it comes to that (1:10).

+ Paul took it as a given that his ministry would lead to suffering; for him it was simply part of the package (1:12). Do we share that expectation? If not, our expectations need to be readjusted. Those embarking on full-time ministry and those taking on a particular lay ministry within the church need to be taught to expect suffering. Church families need to recognise something of the suffering that goes with ministry so that they can learn to pray for, love and support their pastors.

+ Paul is fundamentally optimistic about the future progress of the gospel (1:12). We should be too. In part, this will help us to see that we are not indispensable in our particular ministry (because God has the future in hand), and so it should encourage us to be willing to hand over our ministry to younger people when the time comes.

+ Gospel ministry is fundamentally a matter of stewardship of the gospel rather than innovation (1:13-14). Being a steward is less glamorous and less headline-catching, but it is essential that all gospel ministers should be willing to heed this calling. We Bible teachers need to be warned of the temptation to make a name for ourselves by finding a new angle on a Bible passage or doctrine. Christian people and congregations need to be wary of seeking leaders who promote new or modified doctrine.

+ All of us must take warning from the fact that so many people deserted Paul (1:15). We must not imagine that, when pressure comes, we would be immune to the temptation to distance ourselves from gospel ministers who are facing opposition and shame.

+ How can we follow the example of Onesiphorus in standing with persecuted gospel ministers and fellow believers? The help he offered Paul was very practical in nature and may well have enabled Paul's very survival. Where are believers in similar need today, and what can we do to help?

Suggestions for preaching

The exhortation to remain faithful to the apostolic gospel must be central here. The material could be divided in a number of ways; below are three initial suggestions. The differences between the three outlines are slight and essentially stylistic. For all three outlines it would be possible to preach and apply the sermon initially to pastor-teachers and then in a derived way to all believers. And whatever outline is used, it would also be possible to showcase the wonder of the life-giving gospel for unbelievers to see (although outline 3 might lend itself most naturally to a context in which a number of unbelievers will be present because the gospel itself is front-and-centre).

Sermon 1

1. The call to gospel faithfulness (1:8, 1:13-14)

2. The motivation for gospel faithfulness

    a. The gospel itself (1:9-10)

    b. Two models of faithfulness (1:11-12, 1:16-18)

Sermon 2

1. A gospel call (1:8, 1:13-14)

2. A gospel confidence (1:9-12)

3. A gospel concern (1:15-18)

Sermon 3

1. Paul's cause – the gospel (1:9-12)

2. Paul's charge

    a. Suffer for the gospel (1:8; with positive and negative illustration from 1:15-18)

    b. Guard the gospel (1:13-14)

Suggestions for teaching

Questions to help understand the text

1. What are the two alternatives Paul presents to Timothy (1:8)? Why must it be either one or the other?

2. Why is God's power relevant here? How has God demonstrated his power (1:9-11)?

3. The gospel summary of these verses is unique in Paul's writings (compare, say, the gospel summary in Rom. 5:1-2). What stands out in this summary?

4. Why has Paul summarised the gospel in the way that he has in this particular passage?

5. What is the nature of the link between Paul's appointment to ministry and his suffering (1:11-12)? Why do they naturally go together?

6. Why is Paul unashamed? [Leaders may wish to explain that the 'trust' here in v. 12 is probably the gospel and not Paul's life.]

7. What is Timothy to do and why (1:13-14)? What would it look like if Timothy failed to do this?

8. Why does Paul speak of the deserters and of Onesiphorus here (1:15-18)? What is the lesson?

Questions to help apply the text

1. In what circumstances will gospel ministers face the temptation to be ashamed of the gospel? In what circumstances will believers in general (rather than ministers specifically) face the temptation to be ashamed?

2. Rather than be ashamed and fall silent, what are we all to do? What might this look like practically for you?

3. How are we to do this? From the passage, what help and encouragement are we given?

4. If we share Paul's confidence about the future of gospel ministry, how will that confidence shape the way we go about any ministry we have a part in, and how will it help us rightly to think about and plan for its future?

5. How can we guard the apostolic gospel in our own lives, in the life of our church, and in any ministry we have a part in? Where are we in danger of modifying the gospel?

6. Do I believe that I could become a gospel deserter? What steps can we take to avoid this danger for ourselves and to encourage each other to keep going in faithfulness?

7. Where are there ministers and fellow believers facing persecution and in need of our help? How can we support them and show solidarity with them?

3

THE SUFFERING GOSPEL SERVANT

(2:1-13)

You then, my son, be strong in the grace that is in Christ Jesus. And the things you have heard me say in the presence of many witnesses entrust to reliable men who will also be qualified to teach others. Endure hardship with us like a good soldier of Christ Jesus. No-one serving as a soldier gets involved in civilian affairs – he wants to please his commanding officer. Similarly, if anyone competes as an athlete, he does not receive the victor's crown unless he competes according to the rules. The hardworking farmer should be the first to receive a share of the crops. Reflect on what I am saying, for the Lord will give you insight into all this.

Remember Jesus Christ, raised from the dead, descended from David. This is my gospel, for which I am suffering even to the point of being chained like a criminal. But God's word is not chained. Therefore I endure everything for the sake of the elect, that they too may obtain the salvation that is in Christ Jesus, with eternal glory.

Here is a trustworthy saying:

If we died with him,
   we will also live with him;

> if we endure,
>> we will also reign with him.
> If we disown him,
>> he will also disown us;
> if we are faithless,
>> he will remain faithful,
> for he cannot disown himself.

Introduction

These verses again focus on the theme of suffering, and particularly the suffering involved in enduring toilsome labour for the gospel (especially in the context of opposition). Paul alludes briefly to his own example, but then points to the supreme model of suffering for the sake of the gospel, Jesus Christ himself. While the call to suffer is a hard one, Paul reminds Timothy and us that, as Jesus' suffering was followed by glory, so too will our suffering lead to glory. The reminder that suffering comes before glory for followers of Jesus not only serves as encouragement, it also serves to counter the false teaching that insists that the victorious resurrection age has already arrived.

Listening to the text

Context and structure

The emphatic 'You, then...' that begins this section marks Timothy off from the deserters of 1:15. He is to be distinctive as he holds the line of orthodoxy (1:13-14) and stays faithful to Paul and his message as Onesiphorus did (1:17-18). Faithful guarding of the apostolic gospel will require strength (2:1), commitment to training others (2:2), and a willingness to endure hardship (2:3). All these instructions relate closely together, and they are illustrated by the images of the soldier, athlete and farmer (2:4-6;

the particular instruction to 'endure hardship' is the direct heading for the three illustrations). Living and ministering in this way ultimately reflects authentic discipleship of the Lord Jesus, and so Paul's instruction to 'remember Jesus Christ' (2:8) serves the broader call to endurance and flows naturally from it. Paul shows that he himself has done what he instructs Timothy to do (2:9-10). The 'trustworthy saying' (2:11-13) may be a poem or hymn fragment that was known to believers at the time. Its message, that suffering comes before glory for true believers, flows naturally from the call to remember Jesus, and indeed it helps to the reader to do just that. In the following passage Paul will move on from reminding Timothy of the costly shape of true discipleship and will call him to remind the people under his care of the same thing. This reminder will be of vital importance because there is false teaching circulating in Ephesus that undermines the very truth conveyed in this 'trustworthy saying.'

Working through the text

When the pressure of gospel opposition mounts, Paul knows that the temptation to abandon the apostolic message and desert fellow gospel workers will be immense, and so, in light of his experience of desertion (1:15), Paul calls Timothy to stand firm: **'You then, my son, be strong in the grace that is in Christ Jesus'** (2:1). As elsewhere, the 'you' is emphatic, designed to show Timothy that he is to be utterly distinctive and set apart from the negative examples of unfaithfulness around him (see 3:10, 14; 4:5). Having known the pain of desertion, he is deeply concerned that his 'son' in the faith – his 'dear son' (1:2) – should not join the deserters. Paul knows that Timothy will not have the strength in and of himself to stand, so he calls him to

Stand firm

stand, not in his own strength, but in the strength that is his through his union with Christ. Like at 1:2, the 'grace' that is in view here encompasses the redeeming grace that is the basis of the believer's union with Christ, and the sustaining grace that God provides through that union and by his Spirit. Here in 2:1, the context indicates that the emphasis falls particularly on the latter, that is, on the sustaining grace of God in Christ. Again and again, Paul gives instruction alongside the reminder that God himself supplies the resources to enable what he requires.

Timothy's task does not extend merely to holding the line of orthodoxy himself; faithful gospel stewardship will require him to plan and prepare for the future of gospel ministry. He must take the apostolic gospel he has heard Paul **'say in the presence of many witnesses'** (that is, 'the good deposit' entrusted to him, 1:14) and **'entrust [it] to reliable men who will also be qualified to teach others'** (2:2). Timothy is to give the necessary time and energy to train 'reliable' and 'qualified' men of the kind described in 1 Timothy 3:1-7 who will be able to teach others. Notice the scope of Paul's vision. He is concerned about the future health of the church and the continuation of gospel ministry, not simply for the next year or decade, but for the coming generations. He has four generations of gospel ministry in view even here in this verse.[1] He is continuing his own ministry in the writing of this letter (one generation). He is training and equipping Timothy for his ministry through the letter (a second generation). He is urging Timothy to equip a further generation of gospel ministers (a third generation),

---

1   I owe this observation to Peter Adam (2 Timothy – the Making of the Man of God: address given at the Proclamation Trust Senior Ministers' Conference 2001. Audio available online at www.proctrust.org.uk.).

who will in turn be able to hand on the gospel to others (a fourth generation). Paul has a far-reaching concern for the future preservation and proclamation of the true gospel.

The instruction to hand the gospel on to others is framed by the dual call to 'be strong' (2:1) and 'endure hardship' (2:3). This is no mistake or coincidence. The work of discipling others and training them for ministry requires great strength and will be costly in many ways. As we see from Paul's own discipleship and training of Timothy, it takes an enormous investment of time and emotional energy to encourage and develop future leaders. For Paul, such mentoring was never merely a classroom exercise; it was always grounded in a deep sharing of life. Timothy was not only Paul's protégé, but his 'dear son' (1:2). Paul took the trouble to write to Timothy, and he prayed for him 'constantly','night and day' (1:3). His affection for Timothy was so sincere that he longed to see him, and he knew that their reunion would fill him with joy (1:4).

In his commentary on 2 Timothy, John Stott makes grateful mention of E. J. H. Nash: 'I thank God for the man who led me to Christ and for the extraordinary devotion with which he nurtured me in the early years of my Christian life. He wrote to me every week for, I think, seven years. He also prayed for me every day. I believe he still does. I can only begin to guess what I owe, under God, to such a faithful friend and pastor.'[2] Following the example of the Apostle Paul and modelling obedience to the instruction of 2 Timothy 2:2, Nash exercised an extraordinary ministry to young men through the summer camp he led, and many of these men went on to positions of significant leadership and wide influence in Gospel ministry.

---

2   Stott, *Message*, p. 29.

In the case of Paul's ministry to Timothy and investment in him, there was much cause for Paul to be encouraged. But his investment in other potential leaders had been much more disappointing. He knew the pain of widespread desertion by 'all in the province of Asia' (1:15), and we can only imagine how many people in that region Paul had invested in. More specifically, Paul speaks later of Demas' desertion 'because he loved this world' (4:9). The reality is that this costly work of discipleship and training will not always be fruitful, and it will occasionally end in heartache. That is at least part of the reason why Timothy will need God's gracious strengthening for the work, and why he will need to be prepared to endure hardship.

Paul's call to **'endure hardship'** alongside him (2:3) in the work of gospel ministry generally, and of training up future leaders especially, is now illustrated by appeal to three different types of vocation, each of which is exacting in its own way and each of which has an ultimate goal or prize in view. This future-orientated perspective anticipates Paul's appeal to the example of Jesus (2:8) and his citation of the 'trustworthy saying', which reminds us that suffering in the present will give way to glory in the future (2:11-13).

The first demanding vocation which offers a parallel to ministry is that of a soldier: **'Endure hardship with us like a good soldier of Christ Jesus. No-one serving as a soldier gets involved in civilian affairs – he wants to please his commanding officer'** (2:3-4). Like the gospel minister, the soldier is concerned to serve and please the person under whose authority he operates, hoping ultimately to receive his approval.[3] For the believer, our 'commanding officer' is,

---

3   The term rendered by the NIV 'commanding officer' literally means 'enlisting officer', but the difference is slight, and the point is that the soldier wishes to please the one to whom he is responsible and under whose authority he operates.

of course, the Lord Jesus himself. The Christian aims to receive his commendation, 'Well done, good and faithful servant' (Matt. 25:21, 23).

The soldier knows that duty will require him to forego certain civilian pursuits while he is in active service. He must remain focused and not allow himself to be distracted by activities and pleasures which are harmless in themselves and normal for most people to engage in, but which would draw him away from the task at hand. To allow himself to be distracted in that way would disqualify him for military service. Similarly, the pastor-teacher knows that there is a difference between him and even the rest of the Christian family. He has been set apart for prayer and the ministry of the word. For the sake of his ministry he will have to make sacrifices in order to remain focused. And for the believer who is entrusted with any Bible-teaching ministry (even if not full-time or in an 'ordained' capacity), that ministry will require the sacrifice of other pursuits and activities to ensure that the ministry is not undermined.

When considering this teaching it is important not to go beyond the text in drawing conclusions that would set this passage at odds with what Paul teaches elsewhere about the nature of the calling of a pastor-teacher. Some have taken verse 4 to mean that ministers must not marry. Paul makes it clear elsewhere that marriage would be his right as a gospel minister and apostle, but that he has freely chosen to set that right aside (1 Cor. 9:5). It would be easy to conclude that gospel ministers should not have any paid work alongside what they receive from their ministry. But while that may be the ideal, for some it is not practical, and again Paul himself provides a model of self-support through secular employment (Acts 18:1-4, 20:33-35).

This is not a command for the pastor-teacher to have no other interest or to engage in no other activity beyond teaching the Bible. The point is to set aside any distraction that would undermine the ministry. Arguably having no other interest or diversion would be so psychologically unhelpful that such a one-dimensional person would be quite unable to minister effectively! Paul wisely refrains from legislating specific applications and out-workings of this principle, but he has confidence that as Timothy reflects on what he is saying, 'the Lord will give [him] insight into all this' (2:7).

The imagery now moves to the world of sport: **'Similarly, if anyone competes as an athlete, he does not receive the victor's crown unless he competes according to the rules'** (2:5). The image of the Christian life as a race is not unfamiliar (Phil. 3:13-14; Heb. 12:1-2), but the unique element here is the emphasis on competing **'according to the rules'.** The rules in view are not specified. It could be a general reference to refraining from cheating, so that the application would be for the gospel minister to conduct his ministry with integrity. The problem with that interpretation is that it does not fit easily with the immediate context, where the emphasis is on strength and endurance. It seems more likely that Paul refers here to the ancient requirement that those who took part in the Olympic Games should swear on oath that they had undertaken strict training for ten months prior to the start of the Games.[4] Only those who put in the long, hard months of daily training could expect to take part in the Games, let alone receive the victor's crown. As with the previous image, a final goal is in view here, this time the wreath crown of the winner in a race. Paul has

4   Kelly, J.N.D., *A Commentary on the Pastoral Epistles* (London, UK:A&C Black, 1963), p. 176.

spoken elsewhere of the people who have been converted and discipled under his ministry as his 'crown' (Phil. 4:1; 1 Thess. 2:19), and his focus here is on the final accounting when the Lord evaluates a gospel minister's labours.

The final image makes a similar point about the necessity for disciplined hard work, and the reward that will accompany it: '**The hardworking farmer should be the first to receive a share of the crops**' (2:6). Whether the implication is that the hardworking peasant farmer will receive a share of the crops before the owner of the land or before other, less industrious farmers, is not clear. But the point that only hard work leads to reward is plain enough. Unlike Paul's use of agricultural imagery in 1 Corinthians 9:7-12 and 1 Timothy 5:18, there is little ground from the context to see the reward here in material terms as the financial support due to a hard-working gospel minister. The focus throughout the three images, in line with the 'trustworthy saying' of 2:11-13, is eschatological. Paul has in view the reward and commendation that the Lord will give his faithful servants at the final day.

The broad point of these three images is that the gospel minister must give himself diligently to the hard work required for his ministry, and endure the cost and hardship that his labour may entail. The precise implications of this basic principle for each minister will vary. Paul does not legislate specifics here, but he calls Timothy and all who follow to '**reflect on what I am saying, for the Lord will give you insight into all this**' (2:7).

Paul's next instruction to '**remember Jesus Christ**' (2:8) follows naturally from the call to labour self-sacrificially for the gospel. The false teachers in Ephesus who spoke of living in the full victory of resurrection life in the here and now (2:18) conveniently forgot all about the real Jesus, who suffered and died before he rose, and who called his followers to do the same: 'If anyone would come after me, he must deny himself and take up his cross and follow me. For whoever wants to save his life will lose it, but whoever loses his life for me and for the gospel will save it' (Mark 8:34-35). Paul wants Timothy to remember the real Jesus who – despite the fact that he was the '**Christ**', the promised King '**descended from David**' – nonetheless had to be '**raised from the dead**' because he willingly suffered for the sake of his people. Paul reminds Timothy that the gospel of a King who died before he rose is '**my gospel**' (2:8) – the true, apostolic gospel – and it is the gospel for which he is '**suffering even to the point of being chained like a criminal**' (2:9). Remembering this real Jesus of the authentic gospel not only counters the false gospels circulating in Ephesus, it also provides the basis of Paul's expectation that he and Timothy should suffer in service of Jesus and the gospel.

Paul's willingness to suffer is further strengthened by his confidence that the work of God will continue through the proclamation of the powerful word of God, which '**is not chained**', even if he its messenger is chained at present. With this confidence Paul is willing to '**endure everything for the sake of the elect, that they too may obtain the salvation that is in Christ Jesus, with eternal glory**' (2:10). Again, Paul's eschatological focus shines through. Here his concern is not with any reward that he may gain, but with the salvation that those who sit under his ministry will enjoy. The implication is simply that any suffering that the gospel minister is called to endure is amply justified by the eternal consequences of his work. The call for Timothy to suffer in his labour for the gospel is grounded in the work of Jesus (and thus in the very substance of the gospel) and buttressed by the example of Paul.

The 'trustworthy saying'[5] that follows supports all that Paul has been saying so far in chapter 2 and it grounds his exhortations firmly in the historical work of Jesus and the prospect of his final judgment. For gospel ministers, as for all believers, our life and ministry are to conform to the shape of Jesus' life and ministry: it is suffering now, glory later.[6] This is genuine Christianity. False gospels will regularly claim that the promise of the gospel is suffering never, glory now (see 2:18). But if in accepting the true gospel we have decided to follow Jesus' example in dying to self, we can expect to **'live with him'** (2:11). If we faithfully **'endure'** hardship and suffering in the present (see 2:3), we can expect to share his final heavenly **'reign'** (2:12a). The fact that believers will reign over the new creation with the Lord Jesus is rarely discussed, but is a clear teaching of Scripture (Dan. 7:18, 27; 1 Cor. 6:2; Eph. 2:6; Rev. 22:5), and a truly glorious prospect. For gospel workers like Paul and Timothy who faced opposition, marginalisation and worse, the reminder that they would ultimately share in the triumphant universal reign of the Lord Jesus is more than sufficient encouragement to carry them through discouraging days. And in the current climate where the

---

5   This is one of five 'trustworthy sayings' in the Pastoral Epistles (the others are found at 1 Tim. 1:15, 3:1, 4:9 and Titus 3:8). The phrase 'trustworthy saying' probably serves primarily to mark the truth and reliability of the statement, and possibly indicates that it is a traditional saying that has been in wider circulation and should be accepted as valid. See further discussion in Marshall, I.H., 'The Pastoral Epistles', International Critical Commentary (London: T&T Clark International, 1999), pp. 326-30, 397.

6   I owe the summary of the message of this section as 'suffering now, glory later' to my colleague Christopher Ash.

gospel is increasingly marginalised and disdained in many parts of the world, that same reminder is a powerful encouragement for us.

However, there is a negative counterpart to this. If we refuse to die to ourselves and refuse to suffer, and instead **'disown him'** (as others have done and are in danger of doing; 1:15, 2:17, 4:10), we must know that **'he will also disown us'** (2:12b) when it comes to the final judgment. The next stanza reinforces this stark warning. Even if we are faithless in character, the Lord Jesus is always faithful, true and consistent to his word. The promise of 2:12 will be carried through if we fail to heed the warning. He will indeed disown the apostate. To that commitment **'he will remain faithful, for he cannot disown himself'** (2:13). This final stanza of the trustworthy saying is thus a stark warning: the unfaithful, apostate person will face the judgment of God.

The eschatological focus of this 'trustworthy saying' as a whole sharpens Paul's exhortations to Timothy. Positively, it adds great encouragement, reminding Timothy that there is a glorious future in store for those who remain faithful to Jesus and his gospel. Negatively, there is a sobering reminder that the Lord will judge those who shrink back from costly service through disowning him.

From text to message

Theme and aim

It does not seem necessary here to offer a separate aim for the pastor teacher and for the church as a whole. Because the call of these verses is so firmly and explicitly grounded in the example of Jesus and in the very nature of the gospel, there should be quite direct lines of application here for every believer. If anything, the nature of the differences between applications for the pastor-teacher specifically and for the believer in general may be in their degree rather than their basic character. If the pastor-teacher is called to endure particular hardship for the gospel, it is as a model and as a leader, but not as an exception to this gospel-shaped pattern of costly service.

Theme:	For gospel ministers, like Jesus, there is suffering before glory.
Aim:	Endure hardship for the gospel in light of the coming glory.

A way in

The preacher might begin: 'It is very easy for us to buy into the comfortable myth that Jesus basically wants to make our lives easier – to make us happy, and to take away our troubles. Jesus offers us an unimaginably bright future, to be sure. But Paul wants to remind us in these verses that, in the Christian life generally (and in gospel ministry especially), the pattern is suffering first, glory later.'

Ideas for application

+ Look for leaders who are willing to suffer and labour for the gospel and who understand that gospel ministry will involve hardship.

+ Pray for gospel ministers to stand firm in the grace of Jesus when suffering comes, and encourage them with the reminder of that grace.

+ Gospel ministers need to be realistic about the fact that ministry will involve hardship, and not be surprised when it comes.

+ Gospel ministers need to be prepared to work hard. This must not be used as a licence to ignore other God-given responsibilities, especially family responsibilities.

+ Leaders set the model for this in churches, but the pattern of suffering for the gospel is the basic pattern that Jesus set for all his disciples, so all believers should expect to share in suffering for the gospel, especially in the context of any areas of gospel ministry where they serve.

+ Training future leaders for gospel ministry is a vital priority. It will take hard work and will be costly. We need to share Paul's concern for future generations. If you are a gospel minister, are you giving time to this work? If you have some form of Bible teaching ministry within the church, do you see the work of training future leaders of that ministry as a priority?

+ We need to remember and proclaim the true Jesus, who died before he rose. Proclaiming consistently the One who died and then rose again will guard us from skewed gospels, like the currently popular prosperity gospels.

+ We need to maintain a proper eschatological focus to sober us and warn us against denying Jesus, and to fill us with the hope of glory – both for ourselves as we hope in the gospel, and for others as we make the good news known.

+ For the unbeliever this passage is a great help in weighing the cost of following Jesus. Becoming a follower of Jesus will lead to suffering. Are you willing to bear the cost?

Suggestions for preaching

Below are two possible outlines for preaching this passage.

Sermon 1

The first sermon outline is very simple and stands back from direct application in its headings. This will probably give the most scope for offering a range of applications to a whole church family.

Paul's call to Timothy:

1. A call to endure (2:1-7)

2. A call to remember (2:8-13)

Sermon 2

This second outline breaks the passage down into four parts and moves more directly to application; however, it should still give scope for offering application to people in a range of situations, and it need not imply an assumption that everyone is a 'Timothy'.

Paul's strategy for the future:

1. Be strong in the gospel (2:1)

2. Entrust the gospel to others (2:2)

3. Endure hardship for the gospel (2:3-7)

4. Remember the gospel (2:8-13)

Suggestions for teaching

Questions to help understand the text

1. In light of the previous verses, what is the concern motivating Paul's charge in verse 1?

2. How is Timothy to 'be strong'? What will this involve?

3. What is Paul calling Timothy to do in verse 2, and why?

4. How does the call of verse 3 relate to verses 1 and 2?

5. What is the theme running through the three images (2:3-6)? What is the lesson of the three images?

6. Why the instruction of verse 7?

7. Why does Paul call Timothy to 'remember Jesus' (2:8)? Surely Timothy has not forgotten him! What does Timothy need to remember about the true Jesus?

8. Why is Paul willing to suffer and endure (2:8-10)?

9. What does the 'trustworthy saying' (2:11-13) teach us, and how does it relate to verses 1-10?

Questions to help apply the text

1. Why does faithful gospel ministry require strength and the endurance of hardship? How can we support and pray for gospel ministers more effectively in light of this passage?

2. What will it look like for us to be strong in the redeeming and sustaining grace of God in Christ? How can we heed this instruction personally, and how can we encourage others to heed it?

3. In light of this passage, what are some characteristics of a godly gospel minister? In what circumstances will we need to remember this?

4. To the extent that we have ministries for which we are responsible, are we:

    (a) prioritising the work of training up future ministers?

    (b) willing to endure hardship and prepared for hardship?

    (c) working hard?

5. In what ways are we in danger of forgetting the true Jesus and the authentic gospel? Have we come to believe, even in some small way, that Jesus' job is to make our lives easier and more pleasant?

6. What are we unwilling to endure for the sake of the gospel?

7. Are there particular pressure points where we sense the danger that we might be faithless or even disown Jesus? How can we pray for each other in this area?

4

THE UNASHAMED GOSPEL WORKMAN

(2:14-26)

Keep reminding them of these things. Warn them before God against quarrelling about words; it is of no value, and only ruins those who listen. Do your best to present yourself to God as one approved, a workman who does not need to be ashamed and who correctly handles the word of truth. Avoid godless chatter, because those who indulge in it will become more and more ungodly. Their teaching will spread like gangrene. Among them are Hymenaeus and Philetus, who have wandered away from the truth. They say that the resurrection has already taken place, and they destroy the faith of some. Nevertheless, God's solid foundation stands firm, sealed with this inscription: "The Lord knows those who are his", and, "Everyone who confesses the name of the Lord must turn away from wickedness."

In a large house there are articles not only of gold and silver, but also of wood and clay; some are for noble purposes and some for ignoble. If a man cleanses himself from the latter, he will be an instrument for noble purposes, made holy, useful to the Master and prepared to do any good work.

Flee the evil desires of youth, and pursue righteousness, faith, love and peace, along with those who call on the Lord out of a pure heart. Don't have anything to do with foolish and stupid arguments, because you know they produce quarrels. And the Lord's servant must not quarrel; instead, he must be kind to everyone, able to teach, not resentful. Those who oppose him he must gently instruct, in the hope that God will grant them repentance leading them to a knowledge of the truth, and that they will come to their senses and escape from the trap of the devil, who has taken them captive to do his will.

Introduction

Having charged Timothy to 'guard the good deposit' (1:14) of the apostolic gospel and to 'remember Jesus Christ' as he really was and is (2:8), Paul now turns to address the question of how to avoid distorted gospels and those who teach them. He will insist that Timothy and all believers avoid the kind of theological discussion that allows heresy to take hold. He will also call Timothy to invest time and effort in instructing misguided but pure-hearted believers who oppose him.

Listening to the text

Context and structure

The previous section (2:1-13) constituted a positive call to remain faithful to the apostolic gospel. These verses continue that call, but turn the focus toward remaining faithful by responding rightly to error. Verses 14-19 will focus on avoiding the kind of conversation and debate that leads to error. Verses 20-21 provide an illustration to underpin the teaching point made in verses 14-19. In verses 22-26 Paul gives principles for approaching and maintaining godly inter-personal relationships in the context of theological conflict. The verses that follow at the opening of chapter 3 will address the right approach to take when the opponents are unconverted and particularly dangerous, and where personal separation is necessary.

Working through the text

In verse 8, Paul has called Timothy to remember the true Jesus who – although he was the Christ, the kingly descendent of David – died before he rose. The pattern Jesus set applies to all his disciples: in the Christian life, it is suffering now, glory later (2:11-13). Paul now instructs Timothy to **'keep reminding them of these things'** (2:14). That is, he is to keep reminding the church under his care (who are, of course, listening in; see 4:22 and comments) of the authentic Jesus. They will need to be reminded of the true Jesus of Paul's gospel because of the false gospel that has infiltrated the church at Ephesus (2:18). As a further defence against error, Timothy is to **'warn them before God against quarrelling about words'** (2:14). It is not immediately clear what Paul means by 'quarrelling about words'. This unusual verb does not itself give us a precise pointer here, but the context helps us immensely. Although this is obscured in the NIV, in the Greek of verse 14 the primary instruction is to 'remind them', while the call to 'warn them' (a participle) is presented as a component part of that broader instruction: 'Remind them of these things, warning them not to quarrel about words...' (trans. mine). The two activities, then, of reminding them and warning them relate closely. An indulgence of the desire to quarrel about words will move the participants away from a true memory of the real Jesus and of the apostolic gospel.

Further, whatever it is to quarrel about words, we know that **'it is of no value, and only ruins those who listen'** (2:14). 'Quarrelling about words' is not edifying, and it leads people away from the truth, into theological error, and so spiritual ruin. The call to Timothy in verse 15, to handle the word rightly and with integrity, is quite clearly a call to stand out in contrast to this kind of behaviour. So, we may take 'quarrelling about words' as an approximate opposite to 'correctly handling the word of truth'. Presumably 'quarrelling about words' is the same behaviour described as 'godless chatter' in verse 16. It is exemplified, ultimately, by Hymenaeus and Philetus, who have wandered into error and are espousing a false gospel (2:17-18; note that the term 'quarrels about words' is a typical behaviour of disruptive and ungodly teachers of false doctrines at 1 Tim. 6:4).

So, we can see that 'quarrelling about words' is a kind of conversation that leads away from the true gospel toward theological error. With that in mind, we might imagine that Paul could simply have called Timothy and the believers at Ephesus to avoid 'false teaching' or 'theological error'. However, presumably his use of the phrase 'quarrelling about words' is intentional and shows us something significant about the road to error and apostasy. Indulging in debates about doctrine which are 'in the end purely verbal, having nothing to do with the realities of the Christian religion'[1] – what Paul will later describe as 'foolish and stupid arguments' (2:23) – never benefits those who participate. Such arguments are never conducted in a spirit of submission to the word of God, but in a spirit

---

1   Kelly, *Pastoral*, p. 182.

of intellectual competitiveness. They may showcase the speaker's intellectual and verbal alacrity, but they never magnify Christ. These kinds of discussions are easy to start and seem harmless at first. But Paul issues a warning against them, seeing how easily they lead to error and apostasy.

Paul's next instruction for Timothy concerns his own faithfulness as a Bible teacher: '**Do your best to present yourself to God as one approved, a workman who does not need to be ashamed and who correctly handles the word of truth**' (2:15). As so often in the letter, Paul's focus here is eschatological. Timothy is to have in mind the final day when he 'presents himself' to God. In light of that day, he is to labour faithfully at his Bible teaching so that he need not feel ashamed when his work is evaluated. The key to being unashamed then is faithful handling of the word now. The term rendered 'correctly handles' literally means to 'cut straight' or 'divide straight'. The precise background and intended imagery of the language is unclear. It evokes some form of manual labour, possibly a carpenter and his saw. But the point is clear enough: Timothy and the Bible teachers who will follow him are to handle the word of God in a careful, skilful and accurate way.

The imagery of 'cutting straight' provides a clear contrast to the false teachers who begin by indulging in 'quarrels about words' and 'godless chatter' – that is, speculative theological debate and discussion about non-central issues. They do not cut the word straight, and the result is that they 'wander' or 'swerve' (esv) away from the truth (2:18). Timothy is to stay on the straight line of the Bible's main gospel themes. It is as though he sees a red line running right through the whole of the Bible – the line of the person and work of Jesus, his promise-fulfilling and sin-bearing death and resurrection. That's the main line of the Bible's story and the focus of God's concern. Timothy is to stay on the line in proclaiming Christ, and him crucified, from all Scripture. He is to stay on message at all times. It is no mere coincidence that the instruction of verse 15 follows directly on from the instruction of verse 14 to 'keep reminding' God's people of 'Jesus Christ, raised form the dead, descended from David' (2:8). Proclaiming him from all Scripture (3:15) is at the heart of what it is to handle correctly the word of truth.

The warning of verse 16 to **'avoid godless chatter'** reinforces the point and provides a contrast to the correct handling of the word that is to characterise Timothy's ministry. Paul's insistence that those who indulge in such chatter **'will become more and more ungodly'** (or, 'will advance to more and more ungodliness') not only serves to underscore the danger of such talk, it also seems to serve as a darkly ironic assault on the self-perception of the false teachers. Three times Paul uses the verb 'to advance' to speak of the failure of the false teachers to achieve true 'advancement' (2:16, 3:9, 3:13). Although we cannot be certain, it stands to reason that the false teachers may have spoken of themselves as the 'advanced', avant-garde teachers and theologians. Probably they saw themselves as moving forward and breaking new ground, while Paul and his unenlightened associates stuck with the same old message and same old theology. If such talk from the false teachers does stand behind Paul's ironic use of the language of 'advancement', it also accounts for his dogged insistence that Timothy should commit himself to being a custodian of the truth rather than a theological innovator (1:13-14, 2:2).

The same temptations exist today, and Bible teachers and preachers urgently need the same caution. The gospel must, of course, be presented and communicated in constantly fresh and innovative ways, but the message itself tolerates no modification. When it comes to the substance of the message, gospel ministers are fundamentally stewards and not innovators. Those who take liberties with the message will advance in only one direction: that of ungodliness and spiritual ruin.

'**Hymenaeus and Philetus**' (2:18) provide a negative example and a warning to Timothy. They probably also provided a prompt for Paul to write as he has written. These men evidently had assumed for themselves some kind of a teaching role within the church and were wielding enough influence as teachers that they were leading others astray (although Paul had evidently already taken steps to excommunicate Hymenaeus, see 1 Tim. 1:20). Paul records with regret the fact that they have '**wandered away from the truth**', implying that they once adhered to the truth and at very least appeared quite orthodox. This fact made them particularly dangerous to the believers in Ephesus ('former evangelicals' are so often the most dangerous opponents).

Their destructive heresy is that '**the resurrection has already taken place**'. This claim refers not to the resurrection of Jesus (which quite clearly has already taken place), but to the resurrection of all believers. They were insisting that the promise of ultimate resurrection and the fulfilment of all God's salvation promises attached to that event had already taken place. Implied in their claim is a denial that the resurrection of believers is a physical event; if it has happened already, it must be an exclusively spiritual reality. In short, the false teachers were promoting the idea that believers were living in heaven on earth. It is a doctrine that re-surfaces with startling regularity, and it is hugely influential in its modern-day manifestations through the various prosperity gospels. Presumably in a place like Ephesus, where money and stimulating cultural experience were in fulsome supply, the lie might have been superficially plausible to some. But even the slightest whiff of suffering must undermine the confidence of believers taken in by this heaven-on-earth heresy, and so the false teachers quickly **'destroy the faith of some'**.

Timothy is to be warned, but he must not fall into despair: **'Nevertheless, God's solid foundation stands firm, sealed with this inscription: "The Lord knows those who are his", and, "Everyone who confesses the name of the Lord must turn away from wickedness"'** (2:19). The Lord's sovereign and eternal purposes are depicted here as an unmovable foundation stone of a great building. On the stone are two inscriptions, both drawn from and recalling the story of Korah's rebellion against Moses and Aaron in Numbers chapter 16. Korah, a Levite, along with a handful of others, gathered 250 leading men from the community of God's people and stirred them up to rebel against Moses and Aaron's authority. They insisted that because the whole of Israel was 'holy', Moses and Aaron had no right to assume for themselves positions of leadership (Num. 16:1-3). After falling face-down, Moses replied to Korah and the others: 'In the morning the LORD *will show who belongs to him* and who is holy...' (Num. 16:5). When the Israelite assembly gathered, the Lord told Moses to warn the people to move away from the tents of Korah and his henchmen: 'Move back from the tents of these wicked men! Do not touch anything belonging to them, or you will be swept away because of all their sins' (Num. 16:26). When Moses finished speaking to the people the earth under Korah and his associates and all their households split open, and they all went down into the earth alive (Num. 16:31-33).

The two allusions to this story are intended to evoke a reminder of the whole episode, and they bring both comfort and warning. The first allusion brings deep comfort to Timothy. Although false teachers like Hymenaeus and Philetus will gain some hearing, ultimately the Lord knows who are his true people and his appointed leaders. Timothy and his ministry will stand if he remains faithful as an approved workman, and the false teachers will perish. There is a warning here too: those who would remain faithful in confessing the name of the Lord 'must turn away from wickedness' (2:19). This recalls the stark warning of Numbers 16:26 that the people must have nothing to do with the doomed rebels – they must not even have physical contact with them, or they will risk likewise being swallowed by the earth (which is a vivid picture of facing God's judgment). The point is clear: God's people are to have nothing to do with these false teachers; it is far too dangerous to associate with them.

Like any good preacher or Bible teacher, Paul pauses now to illustrate what he has been saying. The principle is to maintain separation from dangerous false teachers through avoiding their godless chatter. The image Paul uses is that of a **'large house'** filled with various kinds of **'articles'** or **'vessels'** (2:20). Some of the utensils, goblets and dishes are made of **'gold and silver'** and set apart for **'noble purposes'** (banquets on special occasions), while other pots and pans, jugs and other implements are made of **'wood and clay'** and set aside for ignoble use (perhaps even waste disposal).

The image of the house represents the people of God, the church (see 1 Tim. 3:15, where Paul calls the 'church of the living God', 'God's household'). In particular it represents the *visible* church as we observe it here on earth, which will include both true and false believers. Within that imagery, the 'articles' represent individual people. The people of God who wish to be set apart for noble use must put distance between themselves and ignoble false teachers – Korah in Moses' day and Hymenaeus and Philetus in Timothy's day. **'If a man cleanses himself from the latter, he will be an instrument for noble purposes, made holy, useful to the Master and prepared to do any good work'** (2:21). The implements used at the table for a great banquet must not get mixed up with the implements used for cleaning or waste disposal. That would be a major health risk. The people of God who wish to be useful in the service of God must avoid the godless chatter of the false teachers because it spreads like gangrene. Usefulness requires separation. The imagery assumes that the visible church will be a mixed church, so there will always be a necessary task of discernment in this area. In some times and places the challenge will be greater than in others. Those who serve within churches and denominations that are not uniformly evangelical will know very well the challenge and strain of this task. But usefulness to the Master requires us to be discerning and to be willing to separate ourselves from those who turn away from the truth.

Verses 22 to 26 continue on the theme of dealing with doctrinal error, but here the issue becomes more nuanced. Whereas up until now the message has been simply to avoid the hardened false teachers and the quarrelling about words that leads to error, here the focus is on a different category of opponent (and one who is not clearly taking the role of leader or teacher), and so Paul advocates a different kind of approach. He begins with instruction for Timothy to **'flee the evil desires of youth'** (2:22). Although this instruction is often taken to mean that Timothy should flee the youthful passion of sexual lust, the true meaning is nothing of the kind. Again, the context helps us. Having told Timothy to avoid the unnamed 'evil desires of youth' in the first half of the verse, in the second half of the verse Paul goes on to say what he should pursue: **'righteousness, faith, love and peace, along with those who call on the Lord out of a pure heart'.** Paul will next say that Timothy is to avoid **'stupid arguments'** (2:23), emphasising the fact that **'the Lord's servant must not quarrel'** (2:24). The 'evil desires of youth' that Timothy must flee are the desires and inclinations to pick fights, which are especially (although by no means uniquely) characteristic of younger people.

Rather than fight with the particular opponents in view here, Timothy is to come alongside them and pursue godliness with them. This is a far cry from the call to absolute separation of the previous verses. The reason for this difference in approach is that these are a different kind of opponent.[2] They are **'those who call on the Lord out of a pure heart'** (2:22). Unlike Hymenaeus and Philetus who have gone the way of Korah, arrogantly challenging God's appointed leaders and stubbornly wandering away from the truth, these opponents are true believers who long to know and serve the Lord. They are obviously misguided in some way, but they have not abandoned the truth. With such opponents, Timothy must not argue (even if he feels sorely tempted to do so). Rather, as God's servant, **'he must be kind to everyone, able to teach, not resentful'** (2:24). More

---

2   I owe this observation to Peter Adam; see Adam, *2 Timothy.*

than that, Paul calls upon Timothy to extend his teaching ministry to these people. He is not even allowed to ignore them! Timothy must **'gently instruct'** such people, even as they **'oppose him'**, in the prayerful hope that they might come **'to a knowledge of the truth'** (2:25) and escape **'from the trap of the devil'** (2:26).

It is sobering to note the high stakes that Paul attaches to the confusion and error of the people described in 2:22-26. Although these opponents are true believers, their error and opposition requires 'repentance' (2:25), not simply a 'rethink'. More significantly, in their error and opposition, they have become pawns in the devil's hand; they have been 'trapped' by him and **'taken captive to do his will'** (2:26).

So, then, Paul sets out two broad approaches to these two types of opponent and to their respective brands of doctrinal error. The initial challenge is discernment in terms of identifying which category an opponent may fall into. The greater challenge is pursuing godliness in response.

From text to message

Theme and aim

Theme:	The pastor-teacher must be faithful in handling the word and in addressing error.
Aim (for the pastor-teacher):	Rightly handle the word; respond with godliness to opponents.
Aim (for the church):	Remember the true Jesus; avoid quarrels about words and false teachers.

A way in

We might ask: 'What, to your mind, is the biggest threat to the health and well-being of today's church? What do we need to be on guard against, more than anything else? Perhaps it's the new atheism? Maybe it's the virtual disappearance of Christian moral standards in our society? Or maybe it's the threat of the persecution? I think that if we asked the Apostle Paul what, to *his* mind, was the greatest danger facing the church, he would say this: doctrinal error, false teaching, deviation from the truth. And it's that danger that Paul addresses in the passage before us.'

More narrowly, we might address the theme of false teachers from the start: 'We have probably all seen individual believers and prominent Bible teachers alike who once stood for the truth but who now have wandered away into error. How does such a thing happen, and how do we avoid that danger ourselves?'

It is a regular feature of church life, from time to time, to have to deal with disputes over doctrine. But it is always a difficult thing for church leaders and church members to know exactly how to respond when confronted with teaching that does not faithfully reflect Scripture. Therefore, a third approach for the preacher might be to introduce from the outset the question of how we discern between different types of error and different types of erring teachers, and what constitutes the right response in each case – and to note that Paul addresses that very issue in this passage.

Ideas for application

+ Bible teachers need to 'keep reminding' those they teach of the true Jesus and the true gospel, and the true shape of Christian discipleship. In particular they need to remind them that suffering precedes glory. This reminder will be especially important in an age where the prosperity gospel has taken such a hold in so many places. Faithful Bible teaching ministries will be marked by this regular reminder.

+ All of us need to remember the true Jesus and the true gospel.

+ Bible teachers must warn the people under their care against theological intrigue and dispute that move away from the main gospel themes of the Bible, and each of us must take care not to get caught up in such discussions. We need to heed the warning: if we indulge in this kind of talk, we will become more and more ungodly, and we will risk wandering away from the truth.

+ Where are the particular dangers for us? Which topics of discussion and debate in our church or home group are possible 'quarrels about words' and 'godless chatter'? Where we see it, we need to put a stop to it and repent.

+ Bible teachers must work hard at their Bible teaching to ensure that they are workmen who meet with the Lord's ultimate approval. This means labouring at the text to know what it is really saying; discovering its context within the whole Bible and within its particular Bible book. It means faithfully proclaiming the authentic Jesus from all Scripture. It means working hard at the vocabulary and logic of the passage. It means knowing the people to whom we are speaking well enough to make apt and helpful applications – and applications that will really get under the skin and impact the heart.

+ Congregations should seek Bible teachers who are faithful in this way, and should pray for their teachers to stay faithful (it takes hard work to keep up this faithfulness for the long haul!).

+ Where we see ungodly, truth-denying false teachers at work we need to separate ourselves from them. Leaders and teachers need to take the lead in this. If we refuse to take these costly and difficult steps, we endanger ourselves and others under our care, and we undermine our usefulness to the Master. Are there people from whom we need to separate ourselves in this way?

+ Where do we see the temptation to argue with fellow believers who call on the Lord with a pure heart? Where have we been guilty of doing this? If we are teachers, how can we invest in teaching misguided opponents for the sake of their spiritual good?

+ If you are looking for a new church or a new leader for your church, find a leader who has the courage to take steps of separation from ungodly, truth-denying false teachers, and who also has the grace to bear with and instruct brothers and sisters who oppose him.

Suggestions for preaching

It would be possible to structure a sermon on these verses around the direct instructions Paul gives Timothy. However, that would almost certainly lead to a situation where the whole congregation placed themselves directly in Timothy's shoes, which, of course, would be an unhelpful step to take. A more fruitful approach would be to stand back from the instructions and summarise their key concerns as headings, and then apply those instructions and their implications with precision to various groups within the congregation or study group. 'Faithfulness' is a common theme and central concern in this passage, and the following outline centres on faithfulness as a uniting theme:

1. Faithful remembrance (2:14)

2. Faithful workmanship (2:15)

3. Faithful separation (2:16-21)

4. Faithful peacemaking (2:22-26)

Suggestions for teaching

Questions to help understand the text

1. Of what is Timothy to remind the believers in Ephesus (2:14)?

2. In light of 2:14-19, what does Paul mean by 'quarrelling about words' (2:14)? What has such quarrelling looked like for Hymenaeus and Philetus? How is Timothy to model a godly contrast?

3. What does it mean to be an 'approved workman' and what will be the result (2:15)?

4. What is the heresy of verse 18? Why is it so dangerous?

5. Read Numbers 16:1-34. Paul alludes to verses 5 and 26 of this passage in 2:19. How is Numbers 16 relevant? How does it provide both comfort and a warning to Timothy and to the believers in Ephesus?

6. Read 1 Timothy 3:15. What does the 'house' represent in the image of 2:20? What do you think the 'utensils'

represent? In light of 2:16-19, what is Paul's point in 2:20-21?

7. In light of the broader context of 2:22-26, what are the 'evil desires of youth' that Timothy must flee (2:22)?

8. What is Timothy to avoid? What is he to do – and why (2:22-26)?

Questions to help apply the text

1. Where are we in danger of forgetting the true Jesus? In what ways do we distort our memory of him to make life easier for ourselves?

2. Do we respond well to being reminded of the true Jesus and the true shape of Christian discipleship? Do we seek leaders who remind us? Do we pray for our leaders to be faithful in this way?

3. What are the particular fruitless theological arguments that we have participated in or that we risk indulging in?

4. If you have a Bible teaching ministry, are you taking care to grapple with what the text really says? Where have you become sloppy? Are you staying on the straight line of the gospel themes of the Bible, or do you delight in theological minutiae? What steps can you take to handle the word correctly?

5. Do you seek Bible teachers who handle the word with integrity? Do you pray for your leaders in this area?

6. How are Hymenaeus and Philetus a warning to us? Why is their heresy so dangerous? Where do we see

similar false teaching in the church today? Do we see elements of it in our own circles?

7. Do we seek leaders who are willing and able to separate themselves from ungodly false teachers where necessary? Do we prayerfully support our leaders when and if they have to take such steps?

8. What will it mean for us to 'cleanse ourselves' from ungodly false teachers? What steps do we need to take to do so?

9. If you are a gospel minister, are you making a point of fleeing the youthful desire to argue with other believers? Where do you need to repent and change in this area? Are you investing time and energy in teaching misguided believers who oppose you – or are you simply writing them off?

10. What are the lessons for us in this passage concerning the nature of godly Christian leadership? How will this help us to recognise and prayerfully support godly leaders?

5

TERRIBLE TIMES AND TERRIBLE PEOPLE

$(3:1-9)$

But mark this: There will be terrible times in the last days. People will be lovers of themselves, lovers of money, boastful, proud, abusive, disobedient to their parents, ungrateful, unholy, without love, unforgiving, slanderous, without self-control, brutal, not lovers of the good, treacherous, rash, conceited, lovers of pleasure rather than lovers of God – having a form of godliness but denying its power. Have nothing to do with them.

They are the kind who worm their way into homes and gain control over weak-willed women, who are loaded down with sins and are swayed by all kinds of evil desires, always learning but never able to acknowledge the truth. Just as Jannes and Jambres opposed Moses, so also these men oppose the truth – men of depraved minds, who, as far as the faith is concerned, are rejected. But they will not get very far because, as in the case of those men, their folly will be clear to everyone.

Introduction

Paul continues to address a theme which has been in view since 2:14: the right attitude and approach to those who teach and believe false doctrine. He has already established that there are some false teachers from whom the godly leader must separate (2:16-21), and some opponents who are misguided but genuine in their commitment to Christ, and are therefore people in whom the godly leader must invest time and energy (2:24-26). But lest Timothy and the believers at Ephesus leave this subject with only a message of conciliation ringing in their ears, Paul returns again to a warning against associating with ungodly false teachers. His overview of the ungodly characteristics of these opponents serves also as a subtle rebuke and self-diagnostic for Timothy and the other believers.

Listening to the text

Context and structure

Paul has just taught Timothy how to respond to opponents who 'call on the Lord out of a pure heart'. The strong start to 3:1, 'But mark this....', introduces an urgent warning that there will be other, more dangerous opponents in the season of the last days who will require different treatment. Verses 1-5 give a general characterisation of the kind of ungodly person who will appear in the last days. Verses 6-9 speak particularly of those (probably a sub-section of the larger group described in general terms in 3:1-5; 'For among them are those...', 3:6, ESV) who would seek to exercise influence over others to lead them astray. The characterisation of these opponents serves not only to warn Timothy and the believers to avoid them, it also serves to warn them not to be like them. Thus Paul will begin the next section with a charge to Timothy to be distinctly unlike the people he has just described, and instead to emulate Paul's own example of godliness (3:10).

Working through the text

Paul's opening charge to **'mark this'** (3:1) is the equivalent of underlining in red the verses that follow. He has been at pains to encourage Timothy to avoid the youthful inclination to pick fights and to guard him from sinfully writing off misguided believers who oppose him. But now Paul wants to impress upon Timothy the fact that there will be other opponents with whom he must take an altogether different line.

The appearance of these people will be a characteristic of **'the last days'**. These are not exclusively the days of the immediate lead-up to the return of Christ (as though the appearance of such people will tell us that Jesus will come at any moment now). Rather the phrase 'the last days' refers more broadly to the final stage of salvation history. When the Holy Spirit is poured out at Pentecost in Acts 2, Peter explains to the baffled crowd that the coming of the Spirit is a sign that they have entered the final stage of God's salvation plan. He quotes from Joel's prophecy: 'In the last days, God says, I will pour out my Spirit on all people. Your sons and daughters will prophesy, your young men will see visions, your old men will dream dreams' (Acts 2:17, quoting Joel 2:28). Peter was not saying that the gift of the Spirit was an indication that the judgment would come very soon and at any moment; it was simply a sign of the dawn of a new and final era in God's plans.

In a similar way, the writer of Hebrews characterises this present era as 'these last days': 'In the past God spoke to our forefathers through the prophets at many times and in various ways, but in these last days he has spoken to us by his Son....' (Heb. 1:1-2). The 'last days' are the days in which God has spoken through the person and work of his Son, rather than by prophets who predicted the Son's definitive work.

Paul's point here in 2 Timothy 3 is that the appearance of these ungodly people will be a feature of the final era of God's salvation plan, 'the last days'. In all likelihood there will be seasons when these people will be more evident than in others, but their appearance at regular intervals is to be expected in this period between the two comings of Christ. The description that follows of the characteristics of these ungodly people is wide-ranging in scope, and the overall portrait that emerges is unattractive and unsettling. The traits listed are all indisputably ungodly, although some feel more extreme than others. The individual characteristics probably require little comment, but it is worth noting a uniting feature of the list (a feature which resonates with other parts of the letter): these ungodly people have a deep-seated problem of the heart. Specifically, their *love* is misdirected. They are **'lovers of themselves'**, **'lovers of money'** (3:2), **'without love'**, **'not lovers of the good'** (3:3), **'lovers of pleasure rather than lovers of God'** (3:5). The ugly behaviour that these people exhibit has its root in the affections and deep loyalties of the heart. Paul makes a similar point with reference to Demas, his former co-worker, in chapter 4. Paul remarks that there is an award awaiting him and all those 'who have longed [literally, 'loved'] [Christ's] appearing' (4:8). He then goes on in the following verses to note with sadness that Demas has deserted him 'because he loved this world' (4:9-10). In light of these observations and warnings it is sobering to read later in the Book of Revelation that the church in Ephesus – the same church in view in 2 Timothy – is rebuked because it has 'forsaken' its 'first love' (Rev. 2:4).

The people depicted here in 3:1-5 are dangerous not simply because they are ungodly; they are dangerous because they claim to be believers and have about them an air of superficial plausibility, **'a form of godliness'** (3:5). This is perhaps the greatest shock of this section. So far the description of this group of people has read as a portrait of a pagan society that has turned particularly ugly. But now in verse 5 Paul makes it clear that his description is not of 'the world out there' in terrible times, but of the professing and visible church in terrible times. These people know how to make the right noises and to behave as they should when others are looking. But their godliness is only superficial. They have 'denied' the 'power' of the gospel and of God's Holy Spirit to transform them.

With such people there is only one response to make: **'Have nothing to do with them.'** Remember that Paul is addressing Timothy in the first instance. As a Christian leader it is especially vital that he should put distance between himself and such people because they have the potential to influence and damage the people under Timothy's care. Clearly some of them will seek to do just that: **'For among them are those who creep into households….'** targeting those who vulnerable, immature and easily influenced, and seeking to **'gain control over'** them (3:6-7).

In his description of the targets of these ungodly false teachers Paul fires a warning shot for the congregation who are listening in. The people who are at particular risk are **'weak-willed'** (3:6), **'always learning but never able to**

acknowledge the truth' (3:7).[1] Implicit here is a warning to those who refuse to embrace settled conviction about the truth of the gospel. They are always 'seekers' and 'enquirers', but never committed disciples. Such people should be warned that there is no neutral ground when it comes to the truth of the gospel. If they will not embrace the truth, they will remain vulnerable to charlatans who will gladly sell them lies and half-truths that will bring them to ruin. Paul also notes that these vulnerable people are **'loaded down with sins and...swayed by all kinds of evil desires'** (3:6). That is, they lack godliness and self-control. They may not have really grasped the liberating truth of the gospel that their burden of sin could be dealt with fully and finally (which would certainly fit with their position of susceptibility to false teaching). But in any case, sin had a hold over them, and the warning stands that those who are not godly in life will be all the more susceptible to skewed and dangerous teaching.

These false teachers are compared with **'Jannes and Jambres'** who **'opposed Moses'** (3:8). Jannes and Jambres do not appear in the Old Testament, but they do appear in the Jewish Targums (expansions and commentaries on the Old Testament text) on Exodus 7:10-12 where Moses and Aaron confront Pharaoh's court magicians. There the Targums assign the names Jannes and Jambres to two

---

1   Paul's identification of them as women may, in part, reflect the particular vulnerability of women who worked alone at home during the day and so were easy targets for the false teachers (so Green, *Finishing*, p. 116). Paul uses the diminutive form of the Greek word 'women', with the sense 'little women'. This indicates that he does not have all women in view (so Knight, *Pastoral*, p. 433), but refers specifically to the kinds of women who have the characteristics of weakness he goes on to describe. The application of the implicit warning here should not be restricted exclusively to women, even if it is clearly directed toward a particular group of women in the first instance.

of the court magicians who attempt to perform secret arts to up-stage Aaron and Moses. The Exodus account of the incident makes the point of the comparison quite clear:

> So Moses and Aaron went to Pharaoh and did just as the LORD commanded. Aaron threw his staff down in front of Pharaoh and his officials, and it became a snake. Pharaoh then summoned the wise men and sorcerers, and the Egyptian magicians also did the same things by their secret arts: each one threw down his staff and it became a snake. But Aaron's staff swallowed up their staffs. (Exod. 7:10-12)

The court magicians may have been outwardly plausible as men of spiritual power or insight, but in the final accounting they were shown to be fraudulent and powerless. Ultimately they, like the false teachers at Ephesus, are on the wrong side, 'oppos[ing] the truth' (3:8). The court magicians were rejected and defeated, and these false teachers, 'as far as the faith is concerned, are rejected' (3:9) as well. They are not true believers, despite the 'form of godliness' they affected, and they will be rejected on the final day before God.

More than that, before too long others will recognise that they are charlatans: 'But they will not get ['advance'] very far because, as in the case of those men, their folly will be clear to everyone' (3:9). Like in 2:16 (and later in 3:13), Paul is using the language of 'advancement' and 'progress' (Gk. *prokoptein*) with deep irony. These false teachers no doubt presented their new doctrines as the 'cutting edge' of theology and enticed the gullible to follow them using that pretence. Paul calls their bluff and insists that their 'advancement' will be short-lived and will end in shame.

It is important to see that in this section Paul is not only warning Timothy and the believers at Ephesus to avoid ungodly people like those he has described (although that concern is central here). He is also depicting these ungodly people in vivid terms so that they might act as a mirror before Timothy and the other believers to encourage careful self-examination. It is not immediately clear where Paul is going with his character description nor why he is giving it. Is this a description of society at large, or is it a description of a very compromised church? It is striking that Paul makes his presentation of these people without any initial reference to the attempts of some of their number to teach or lead others. Their 'teaching' role (3:6-7) will only come into view after their character is described (3:1-5). For the first five verses of the chapter (up until the instruction in 3:5b), Timothy and the church with him in are left simply to listen and form an image in their mind's eye of the people described – and feel increasingly uncomfortable as they do so. They would feel uncomfortable because any believer will recognise at least a shadow of himself or herself in this description.

That Paul wants this list to function as a self-diagnostic and gentle rebuke for Timothy (and others) becomes clear in 3:10, where he indicates strongly to Timothy that he should shun the example of the ungodly false teachers and instead imitate Paul's own example ('You, however.....'). We are not given this list that we might point our fingers and shake our heads in disapproval, but that we might repent where our love, like theirs, is misdirected, and where our behaviour is ungodly. That having been said, no true believer could be thoroughly characterised in the way that Paul characterises these people in 3:1-5; they are quite clearly not converted at all (3:8).

From text to message

Theme and aim

Theme:	Ungodly pseudo-Christian people and teachers will appear in the last days.
Aim:	Have nothing to do with such people.

A way in

One approach would be to focus on the idea that we live in 'the last days' and need to be equipped for the challenges that lie ahead for God's people in this particular era: 'World history is made up of a series of stages or epochs, and it is important to know the character of our particular era so that we can know how to live wisely and prudently within it. In many ways it feels like a new era is unfolding at the present time with the marked shift of economic and military power from West to East. As we enter a new era we will need to learn how to adapt. We in the West may need to learn how to live with long-term austerity, and we will certainly need to learn how to live alongside new superpowers in the years to come.'

'Paul and Timothy lived in the early days of a new era – the era brought in by the life, death and resurrection of Jesus Christ. Paul's concern here in 2 Timothy 3 is to equip Timothy to live and minister in this new era with its particular challenges and dangers. And one thing is certain: it is not going to be easy. Verse 1: "But mark this: There will be terrible times in the last days."'

Ideas for application

+ We will see elements of our own hearts and behaviour reflected in the ugly list of 3:1-5. Where do we need to repent? Where are our affections truly set – on the Lord and all that is good, or on ourselves, money and pleasure?

+ For some, these verses may actually show that they have only an outward 'form of godliness' but are not truly converted; the application for them is to repent and trust in Christ. There may be a surprising number of people in this category in any given church, and thus this passage could be an important diagnostic tool with an evangelistic purpose.

+ Believers with a sensitive conscience will easily read this passage and convince themselves that they are not converted. Be careful to show that the people described here are thoroughly characterised by an unregenerate heart and nature. They actively oppose the truth. Reassure true believers that the application of this passage is not that anyone who has failed to reach sinless perfection is unconverted!

+ What steps do we need to take to 'have nothing to do' with those who claim to be believers yet who are like the people of 3:1-5? This will be especially important for gospel ministers to consider on and apply carefully. Given that such leaders surely exist today and hold positions of authority within churches, denominations and educational institutions, it will be a costly and difficult thing for godly leaders to take steps of public separation from them. But that is the clear instruction here.

+ Note that it would be a wrong application of these verses to disassociate ourselves from ungodly people who make no pretence of being Christians (see 1 Cor. 5:9-10). This would rather limit our evangelistic outreach!

+ Are you someone whose grasp of the gospel is weak and who is always learning but never able to come to a knowledge of the truth? Recognise the danger of your position and resolve, with God's help, to reach settled convictions about the truth.

+ If you are a person who fits the description of these verses, take warning: as far as the faith is concerned, you will be rejected if you will not repent.

+ Do not be overly anxious about the progress of false teachers; they are rejected before God, and what they really are will become plain to all in due course.

Suggestions for preaching

However you decide to approach these verses, it would be worthwhile to spend a bit of time dwelling on the portrait of 3:1-5 and allowing its ugliness and its root in the affections of the heart to impact the hearer, before moving on to the application to avoid such people. Paul spends a bit of time painting the portrait and, as argued above, it seems right to assume that he does so in order that Timothy and the believers at Ephesus should examine their own hearts and lives against this rather dark mirror. Once that has been done, then it will be important to move on to the two main lines of application that flow naturally from the passage: warning and encouragement. Here is one suggestion of how the passage could be divided:

+ An ugly portrait (3:1-5a)

+ An urgent warning (3:5b-7)

+ An ultimate confidence (3:8-9)

Suggestions for teaching

Questions to help understand the text

1. Why does Paul begin the description of the people of terrible times with the call, 'But mark this' (3:1)? How do these verses relate to the verses that have come before?

2. What theme runs through the list (note: look for repeated terms) (3:1-5)?

3. What do these people seek to do? Why are they dangerous (3:6-8)?

4. Who are most at risk and why?

5. What is the ultimate end for these ungodly teachers (3:8-9)? [Leaders should take a moment to explain who 'Jannes and Jambres' represent.]

Questions to help apply the text

1. How does reading the description in 3:1-5 make you feel about yourself? What are the right and wrong conclusions to draw from your feelings as you read it?

2. What is the main response Paul commends (3:5)? How do we go about putting this into practice? What would be some wrong ways of putting this verse into practice, and how do we avoid these?

3. Why is this a particular challenge and priority for Christian leaders?

4. What does this passage teach us about the kind of leaders we should seek and avoid? How will it help us to pray for our leaders?

5. What is the warning from 3:6-9? What steps can we take to avoid being those who are taken in by the false teachers?

6. What is the comfort and encouragement that this passage offers the true believer? Why do we need to hear it?

6

KEEPING YOUR BALANCE IN TERRIBLE TIMES
(3:10-17)

You, however, know all about my teaching, my way of life, my purpose, faith, patience, love, endurance, persecutions, sufferings – what kinds of things happened to me in Antioch, Iconium and Lystra, the persecutions I endured. Yet the Lord rescued me from all of them. In fact, everyone who wants to live a godly life in Christ Jesus will be persecuted, while evil men and impostors will go from bad to worse, deceiving and being deceived. But as for you, continue in what you have learned and have become convinced of, because you know those from whom you learned it, and how from infancy you have known the holy Scriptures, which are able to make you wise for salvation through faith in Christ Jesus. All Scripture is God-breathed and is useful for teaching, rebuking, correcting and training in righteousness, so that the man of God may be thoroughly equipped for every good work.

Introduction

Having painted a very unappealing portrait of the ungodly people and leaders who will appear in the 'last days' (3:1-9), Paul now calls Timothy to a very different model of life and ministry, one exemplified by Paul and grounded ultimately in God's word. A godly ministry of this kind will be sustained and equipped by Scripture, and it will be characterised by an unwavering faithfulness to the apostolic, biblical gospel.

Listening to the text

Context and structure

Paul begins this section by drawing a stark contrast with what came before: 'You however, know...' (3:10). He draws Timothy's attention to his own model of godly faithfulness under trial (3:10-11) and notes that it is a model relevant to all believers who seek godliness (3:12). Evil people will continue in their ungodliness, but Timothy is to stand apart from them. Again, a stark contrast is drawn: 'But as for you....' (3:14). The call here is for Timothy to continue in the apostolic and biblical faith he has known. He is to do this because he trusts the integrity of his teachers (3:14) and because he knows the Scriptures (3:15). Paul then reminds Timothy of the sufficiency of Scripture for his ministry (3:16-17), before charging him to proclaim it in the next passage (4:1ff.).

Working through the text

The false teachers of the last days who seek to oppose the truth will be marked by ungodliness and will face ultimate rejection before God. Paul's call to Timothy is to uphold a different standard and follow a different pattern of life and ministry, the pattern that Paul himself has lived by: **'You,** however, know all about my teaching, my way of life, my purpose...' (3:10). At every point in Paul's self-description he stands apart from the false teachers. They had a form of godliness but denied its power (3:5); Paul had true godliness, marked by 'faith, patience, love, endurance' (3:10). They taught falsehood (3:8) and were ultimately driven by the love of self, money and pleasure (3:1-4). Paul, by stark contrast, was driven by genuine love for Jesus and his people and was willing to suffer for the truth. Timothy knew his 'persecutions, sufferings – what kinds of things happened to me in Antioch, Iconium and Lystra, the persecutions I endured' (3:11; see Acts 13:50; 14:5, 19).[1] The false teachers are rejected by God (3:8) and will be seen by all as frauds (3:9). By contrast, Paul found that when he faced trials 'the Lord rescued me from all of them' (3:11).

It will be vital for Timothy to remember Paul's example when false teachers come along. False teachers who love themselves, money and pleasure will often show outward success and will impress the undiscerning – especially if they are currently enjoying the lives of wealth and pleasure they seek. Timothy will need to work hard to hold his nerve. This will be especially tough if he is losing the loyalty of fellow believers precisely because he is suffering

---

1   In Pisidian Antioch, where there had been a wide reception for the word (Acts 13:49), '... the Jews incited the God-fearing women of high standing and the leading men of the city. They stirred up persecution against Paul and Barnabas, and expelled them from their region' (Acts 13:50). At Iconium there was a mixed response to Paul and Barnabas and their message, but again things turned hostile: 'There was a plot afoot among the Gentiles and Jews, together with their leaders, to mistreat them and stone them' (Acts 14:5). At Lystra the people were initially so impressed that they wanted to worship Paul and Barnabas as gods but, again, the tide quickly turned: 'Then some Jews came from Antioch and Iconium and won the crowd over. They stoned Paul and dragged him outside the city, thinking he was dead' (Acts 14:19).

for the gospel and therefore showing signs, in their eyes, of weakness and failure. But Paul reminds him that suffering has never been far from him in his own ministry (see again 2:8-13).

More than that, suffering will be part and parcel of life of any true disciple of Jesus: **'In fact, everyone who wants to live a godly life in Christ Jesus will be persecuted...'** (3:12). The false teachers at 2:18 have peddled a message that the Christian life is about victory and the blessings of heaven now. But Jesus is the King who died before he rose (2:8) and who calls his followers to do the same (2:11-13), and so it should be no surprise that true believers who are united with Christ ('in Christ Jesus', 3:12) will face the suffering of persecution, just as Jesus did.

The following verse presents a fascinating contrast to the plight of the believer in verse 12. The lives of 'evil men and impostors' will be markedly different from the persecuted believer. We might have expected Paul to say that they will 'enjoy temporal pleasure and success'. No doubt many wicked people will. But that is not how Paul presents their situation in contrast to that of the believer who is persecuted. They **'will go from bad to worse, deceiving and being deceived'** (3:13). Next to their situation, the plight of the believer who is persecuted for the sake of godliness amounts to going from 'good to better', because suffering is the route to glory for the people of God (2:11-13). Ungodly leaders will be given to deceiving others; ungodly and undiscerning people will be all too quick to listen (see 4:3-4). But both will face the judgment.

The sad irony is that both the false teachers and their ungodly and very willing hearers think they are on the way to something greater. They imagine that their new and adapted doctrine, whatever it may be (quite possibly the same doctrine of 2:18), is progressive and innovative. As in 2:16 and 3:9, Paul here uses the language of 'progress' with dark irony to describe their march toward deception, apostasy and, ultimately, judgment: these '**evil men and impostors**' will, literally, 'advance' or 'progress' '**from bad to worse**' (3:13). They imagine that they are heading for great things, but nothing could be further from the truth.

Paul again calls Timothy to a contrasting pattern of life and ministry: '**But as for you, continue in what you have learned and have become convinced of....**' (3:14). While the false teachers and ungodly hearers will tumble ever deeper into deception as they wander from the truth, Timothy's challenge is to 'continue'. The ungodly and undiscerning will always prize theological innovation. But where biblical truth is concerned, innovation is merely deception disguised. Timothy must stick with truth and bear the embarrassment of being unoriginal and doctrinally old-fashioned. He is to stick with the gospel he once '**learned and [has] become convinced of**' (3:14). The ungodly and 'weak-willed' people of 3:6, who were taken in by the false teachers, were 'swayed by all kinds of evil desires, always learning but never able to acknowledge the truth' (3:7). A key element of their vulnerability was their refusal to allow themselves to become convinced of the truth and to move from *learning* the gospel to *believing* it. Paul knows that Timothy settled his basic gospel convictions some time ago. He simply must hold to those convictions when the winds of heresy blow.

Paul offers Timothy two compelling reasons to hold to his gospel convictions. The first reason is '**because you know those from whom you learned**' (3:14). That is, Timothy knows the godly character of Paul (3:10-11), and he knows the genuineness of the faith of his grandmother and mother (1:5). The faith they passed on to him was confirmed and commended by a godliness of life and character. The gospel in their lives rang true because it bore good fruit. But the lives of the false teachers and their disciples tell Timothy all he needs to know about their doctrine; it is pure deception.

The second reason Timothy must have the confidence to stick with the true gospel is that **'from infancy'** he has **'known the holy Scriptures, which are able to make you wise for salvation through faith in Christ Jesus'** (3:15). Timothy's deepest confidence comes from the word of God. Timothy has seen the power of God's word in his own life as that word has brought him to faith in Christ. He has undoubtedly seen the word at work in the lives of others through his ministry countless times as well. And so he must stick with the apostolic and biblical gospel he once received.

It is worth noting that the 'holy Scriptures' (3:15) Paul is referring to here are, of course, the Old Testament Scriptures in the first instance. The New Testament books are in the process of being written – and Timothy has certainly not known those Scriptures 'from infancy' (3:15). The principles of these verses extend to the New Testament books as part of Scripture (see 2 Pet. 3:16), but the initial reference here is to the Old Testament Scriptures, and that fact is significant. The Old Testament Scriptures (and not simply the New) are 'able to make you wise for salvation through faith in Christ Jesus'. They proclaim Christ and the good news of his saving work. Here is a clear reminder of the need to proclaim all of Christ from all of Scripture – and a reminder of the power of doing so.

Verses 16 and 17 are famous verses and rightly so. However, it seems likely that they are not regularly used to make their primary point. Often these verses are used to establish the divine authority of Scripture. That is certainly part of Paul's teaching here and a valid point to draw from these verses; after all, Scripture must be authoritative if it is **'God-breathed'** (3:16). But Paul's primary point is not straightforwardly about the authority of Scripture; it is about the sufficiency of Scripture. Notice what he says: **'All Scripture is God-breathed and is useful for teaching, rebuking, correcting and training in righteousness, so that the man of God may be thoroughly equipped for every good work'** (3:16-17).

The fact that Scripture is **'God-breathed'** underpins and guarantees the fact that it will be **'useful'**. It is useful for every aspect of Christian ministry with the divinely intended result that **'the man of God may be thoroughly equipped'**. Paul is driving home for Timothy the fact that Scripture is the all-sufficient, divinely appointed tool for every aspect of his ministry because, when times get tough and false teachers prosper through peddling an alternative gospel to the biblical gospel, Timothy will be tempted to move away from Bible proclamation. He will be tempted to find another, more palatable gospel outside the Bible in order to stop losing ground to the false teachers. And so he must be warned and encouraged to stick strictly with Scripture. He will only do this if he believes, not only that the Bible is true (it is 'God-breathed'), but that the Bible really works (it is 'useful').

More than that, Paul wants Timothy to be convinced afresh that **'all Scripture'** is true and useful for ministry. Timothy will only keep his balance theologically and will only handle the word rightly if he is immersed in the whole of Scripture and committed to teaching its breadth (not just his favourite bits!). It is likely that many of us have downgraded certain parts of Old Testament Scripture in our teaching ministry because we find them too obscure or difficult. But all of it is useful for our ministry, and we are impoverished if we neglect any element of the powerful tool that God has given us in his word.

Paul is a shrewd mentor. He knows that Timothy is very unlikely ever to adopt a position whereby he denies the truth of Scripture. Probably the false teachers circulating in Ephesus in Timothy's time would have said that they too believed that the Bible was true. But if you listened to them teach and preach, their message would not have come from the Bible. And Timothy's danger was not that he would deny Scripture but simply that he would stop using it. Peter Adam, a retired theological college principal, remarks that the question he would love to be able to ask the graduates of his college in twenty years' time is not, 'Do you believe the Bible?' but 'Are you using the Bible?'[2]

If Timothy is to remain faithful in his ministry, he needs to be convinced that the Bible is all he needs for 'teaching' the people under his care (3:15). All the truth that is needed for sound belief and sound living is found in the Bible. If Timothy is faithful in teaching it, his people will know all they need to know. The Bible is sufficient for 'rebuking'. When Timothy finds that the people under his care have wandered into ungodliness he will discover that God addresses the issue and calls the people to repentance as Timothy opens up the word with the offending parties. When Timothy sees believers turning to theological error,

---

2   Adam, *2 Timothy*.

he needs to know that the Bible will be his all-sufficient tool for 'correcting' them. More than that, as he seeks to encourage men and women at Ephesus and elsewhere to live lives of godliness in accordance with the gospel, he can rely entirely on Scripture there too, because it is all-sufficient for 'training in righteousness'.

Paul insists that Scripture equips 'the man of God'. Of course it is true that Scripture equips all God's people, but Paul's particular interest here (as in the whole of the letter) is the equipping of the pastor-teacher, the leader of God's people. The phrase 'the man of God' is used a number of times in the Bible to refer specifically to God's appointed leader of his people and speaker of his word (see, for example, Deut. 33:1 (Moses), 2 Chron. 8:14 (David), 1 Kings 17:18 (Elijah), and probably 1 Tim. 6:11. Given that Timothy is about to receive the charge to proclaim the word with authority and boldness, it seems right to understand Paul to use the phrase here to designate Timothy as God's appointed leader and spokesman.

From text to message

Theme and aim

Theme:	The pastor-teacher must continue in the gospel because of the integrity of his teachers and the sufficiency of Scripture.
Aim (for the pastor-teacher):	Continue in the biblical and apostolic Gospel, using Scripture in all ministry.

Aim   Seek and prayerfully support
(for the church):   leaders who continue in the
                         biblical gospel.

A way in

If the preacher were in the unusual situation of speaking
primarily to a group of Bible teachers, he might begin
with the anecdote mentioned earlier: 'A retired principal of
a theological college says that the question he would love
to ask his graduating students in twenty years' time is not,
'Do you believe the Bible', but 'Are you using the Bible'.[3]
The greatest danger for a pastor-teacher in the long run
is not that he will stop believing the truth of the Bible (if
that is his current conviction), but that he will stop using
it because he struggles to see the fruit of Bible ministry. In
many cases, pastors will come under pressure from their
church members at one stage or another for the ministry to
be about other things than simply opening up Scripture. In
these verses Paul gives us two compelling reasons to stick
with the Bible in every aspect of gospel ministry.'

Alternatively, if speaking to a regular congregation, the
preacher might begin: 'We will all be aware of a wide range
of needs in our church family. Some people are particularly
discouraged at the moment. Some are struggling with
doubt. Some are facing serious illness. Some people have
drifted away from church, and we fear, away from the Lord
Jesus. We have many friends and family members who do
not yet know the gospel. What should be our strategy as
a church for addressing all these needs and ministering to
all these people? Where do we begin? Paul has some very

---

3   Adam, *2 Timothy*.

good news for us in the passage before us in 2 Timothy; he reports that God has provided for us a fresh, relevant and all-sufficient tool to meet every ministry need in our church. The tool is this: the Bible itself.'

Ideas for application

+ Paul indicates from his own example that authentic gospel ministry will be marked by a godly 'way of life', a steadfast gospel 'purpose', along with 'faith, patience, love, endurance, persecutions, sufferings' (3:10):

  + Do we recognise this model as authentic ministry?

  + Do we look for leaders who will minister in this way?

  + Do we pray for and support our ministers, knowing that their ministry will involve this kind of pressure?

  + If we are pastor-teachers, do we expect to face the kinds of pressures Paul faced?

  + If we are pastor-teachers, as we face persecutions and sufferings, are we doing so with godly faith, patience and love?

+ Do we believe that all who seek to follow Jesus will face persecution? This will come as an awful shock if we see Christianity as a hobby. Bible teachers need to prepare the people under their care for persecution by preaching verse 12. Even though persecution is painful, true believers should give thanks that God has saved us from going 'from bad to worse, deceiving and being deceived' – and ultimately missing out on salvation (3:13) .

+ Do we hunger for theological novelty, and put pressure on our leaders to innovate rather than continue (3:14)? We need to seek leaders who are not trying to be original in doctrine.

+ We need to distinguish between novelty and innovation in doctrine on the one hand, and novelty and innovation in church style and culture on the other. It is surely right and necessary to innovate in the communication of the gospel and, to some extent, in how we 'do church'. But it is never right to innovate when it comes to the core of the gospel. Often we struggle to see the difference.

+ Pastor-teachers need to be willing to be less noteworthy in their ministries through shunning theological novelty. 'Continuing' in the truth will not make you famous.

+ It is right to be instinctively wary of new theological fads; they come and go frequently in the evangelical world.

+ When we are unsure as to the genuineness of a new teaching, it is right to consider the character of those who teach it. How do they compare to the godly people who may have taught you the gospel (3:14)? Is their doctrine commended by a genuine godliness of life?

+ It is possible to crave innovation out of a sense of pride, wishing to feel more advanced in our theology than those who first taught us the gospel. This is a particular danger for younger Christians, who may look back on their first teachers (perhaps in childhood or youth, but not necessarily so) as quaint or simplistic in belief. This inclination can be very deceptive and dangerous. Each of us needs to examine our hearts in this area.

+ Ultimately, all teaching needs to be set against Scripture (3:15). That is the ultimate test, and our absolute doctrinal loyalty must be to the Bible itself.

+ Gospel ministers need to be convinced (and, for those further on in ministry, re-convinced) of the sufficiency of Scripture for every aspect of ministry:

  + It is useful for evangelism ('able to make you wise for salvation...'); the most powerful method of evangelism is the proclamation of Scripture;

  + It is useful for 'teaching' God's people doctrine;

  + It is useful for 'rebuking' those who are wandering into sin;

  + It is useful for 'correcting' error in the church;

  + It is useful for 'training' God's people in living godly lives.

+ Gospel ministers need to be committed to preaching and teaching 'all Scripture' and not simply their favourite parts of Scripture. This will bring freshness to the ministry and will ensure that it is not theologically lopsided.

+ Look for leaders who are convinced of the all-sufficiency of Scripture and who use it in every area of ministry.

+ Pray for your leaders to be thoroughgoing Bible people and to stick with the Bible for the long haul.

+ If you exercise some form of ministry, aim to put the Bible at the centre of what you do and trust the sufficiency of the Bible.

+ Remember that the sufficiency and power of the Bible are grounded in the fact that it is God-breathed. We can therefore trust its truth and power; and we must submit to its authority as well. Give thanks to God for the great gift of his all-sufficient word.

Suggestions for preaching

The central call of this section comes in verse 14: 'But as for you, continue in what you have learned and have become convinced of...' Two reasons are then given: because Timothy knows his teachers, and because Timothy knows the Scriptures. The reminder of his faithful teachers encompasses memory of his grandmother and mother, but more immediately, memory of Paul – and of the personal model he has outlined in 3:10-11 (and applied to the whole church family in 3:12). Thus the central call of the passage provides the comprehensive umbrella for expounding the whole. In most contexts it will be best to leave the central instruction in the abstract in any outline, and then apply it specifically and accurately to particular groups of people within the exposition. One possible structure would be the following:

Two reasons to continue in the true gospel:

1. A heritage of faithful teachers.

2. The gift of God's powerful word.

Suggestions for teaching

Questions to help understand the text

1. Why does Paul begin this passage with the introduction 'You, however....' (3:10)?

2. What is the purpose of Paul's personal example here (3:10-11)? How does his example contrast with that of the people described in verses 1-5?

3. In light of what he have learned about suffering so far in 2 Timothy, why should verse 12 come as no surprise?

4. Why is the condition of the people of verse 13 far worse than that of the believers of verse 12?

5. What is the nature of the contrast introduced in verse 14?

6. Why does Paul remind Timothy to 'continue' (3:14)? Why would Paul fear that Timothy could be tempted not to do this?

7. What are the reasons Paul gives Timothy as a basis for his charge to 'continue' (3:14-15)?

8. What is Scripture able to do (3:15-16)? Why is it so powerful?

9. Who is the 'man of God' (see Deut. 33:1, 2 Chron. 8:14, 1 Kings 17:18 and 1 Tim. 6:11, where the same term occurs)?

10. Why is Paul teaching the message of the sufficiency of Scripture to Timothy here? What concern is driving Paul's teaching at this point?

Questions to help apply the text

1. What characteristics does Paul teach us to look for in faithful gospel ministers in this passage?

2. How will this help us to pray for our ministers?

3. As we share in the work of gospel ministry, what aspects of Paul's model of ministry do we most need to learn? Which do we find hardest to stomach, and why?

4. Do we really believe verse 12? Why do we find it hard to believe it? What will be the consequences if we refuse to believe, or fail to remember, verse 12?

5. How can we encourage our gospel ministers to 'continue' in the true gospel? How might we undermine their determination to do so?

6. For the pastor-teacher, where is the temptation greatest for you to innovate rather than 'continue'? How do the affections or 'loves' of your heart fuel the temptation to deviate rather than continue?

7. Who were some godly people who taught you the gospel? Are there ways in which you have departed from their doctrine? Has this been driven by biblical conviction, or by a desire to innovate?

8. Which aspects of the sufficiency of Scripture do we struggle to believe? Where in our church's life have we stopped using, and therefore trusting, the sufficiency of Scripture? How can we set this right?

7

PREACH THE WORD

$(4:1-5)$

In the presence of God and of Christ Jesus, who
will judge the living and the dead, and in view of his
appearing and his kingdom, I give you this charge:
Preach the Word; be prepared in season and out of
season; correct, rebuke and encourage – with great
patience and careful instruction. For the time will
come when men will not put up with sound doctrine.
Instead, to suit their own desires, they will gather
around them a great number of teachers to say what
their itching ears want to hear. They will turn their
ears away from the truth and turn aside to myths. But
you, keep your head in all situations, endure hardship,
do the work of an evangelist, discharge all the duties
of your ministry.

Introduction

With the charge of 4:2 to preach the word we reach the very heart of this letter.[1] This is Paul's central charge for Timothy, and it is the primary concern driving everything else he says to him. Timothy's guarding of the gospel deposit and continuation in the truth are all expressed and confirmed as he proclaims the word. Paul's teaching concerning the reality of suffering and persecution throughout the letter will only be relevant as Timothy invites opposition through his fearless proclamation of the true apostolic word. These verses outline how Timothy is to go about proclaiming the word, and they prepare him for the kinds of response he will encounter.

Listening to the text

Context and structure

Paul has just reminded Timothy of the sufficiency of Scripture for his ministry. He begins this present passage with a solemn charge to put Scripture to use in his ministry by proclaiming it (4:1-2). Paul teaches Timothy key elements involved in faithful word proclamation (4:2) and then anticipates the negative response Timothy should expect to face (4:3-5). He closes this section with a call to faithful endurance in the work of proclamation (4:5). In the following passage Paul will show from his own life and

---

1   This verse is one of the few places that NIV (1984) capitalises 'Word' outside John 1, presumably because the translators detected an implied reference here to Jesus the personal 'Word' (note that the revised NIV (2011) removes the capitalisation). It seems unlikely that the immediate context gives clear support for this line of interpretation. Within the PT Media Teaching series, 'word' is not capitalised unless there is a clear reference to Jesus the personal 'Word', and so the term is not capitalised here.

ministry that he himself has been faithful in doing what he has called Timothy to do (4:6-8).

Working through the text

Aside from being the central charge of the letter, the charge to **'preach the word'** is at the heart of verses one and two. In verse 1 Paul establishes the context in which he issues the charge and he sets out the theological reality that Timothy must keep in mind as he carries out the charge: **'In the presence of God and of Christ Jesus, who will judge the living and the dead, and in view of his appearing and his kingdom, I give you this charge...'** (4:1). Paul is conscious that he is an authoritative agent of Jesus Christ as his apostle (1:1), and so he recognises that the instruction he is giving to Timothy is ultimately a God-given instruction. He issues it 'in the presence of God and of Christ Jesus', meaning that he does so with Father and Son as his witnesses and his authority. The implication is that Timothy is not at liberty to reject the charge of verse 2.

Should Timothy doubt that fact or underestimate the seriousness of the work he has been given to do, Paul reminds him that the Lord Jesus who calls him to proclaim his word is the same Lord 'who will judge the living and the dead'. And so he issues this charge to Timothy 'in view of his appearing and his kingdom' – that is, in view of Christ's imminent return to actualise the full and visible reality of his kingship over the universe. The judgment that Paul has just mentioned is, of course, the central event of his 'appearing' and the inaugural act of his realised 'kingdom'. Timothy must minister in light of a judgment that will have consequences both for him and for his hearers.

For himself, Timothy must remember that he is accountable to the Lord Jesus for his ministry and his faithfulness in it. Paul ministered with an acute consciousness of this fact. In his well-known farewell to the Ephesian elders in Acts 20 Paul makes it very clear that the reality of the coming judgment has shaped his ministry among them: 'I declare to you today that I am innocent of the blood of all men. For I have not hesitated to proclaim to you the whole will of God' (Acts 20:26-27). Paul had in his mind's eye the day when he would appear before the judgment seat of Christ. He knew it would be possible to appear on that day with blood on his hands if, as a gospel minister, he had shrunk from proclaiming the whole will of God from Scripture. However, because he had spoken the truth in its fullness at Ephesus, he was unafraid as he anticipated that day and the evaluation of his ministry. In his closing charge to the congregation he addresses, the writer of Hebrews reflects this same awareness of the grave responsibility of the leaders of God's people: 'Obey your leaders and submit to them, for they are keeping watch over your souls, as those who will have to give an account' (Heb. 13:17, esv).

The other reason why Timothy must proclaim the word 'in view of his appearing and his kingdom' is that his hearers must themselves be ready for the judgment. The Lord Jesus has 'destroyed death and has brought life and immortality to light through the gospel' (1:10), but the benefits of his death-destroying work are only made available as that gospel is proclaimed and received. The proclamation of that message was the *raison d'être* of Paul's ministry (1:11). But without knowledge of that true message, no one can be ready for the coming judgment. Timothy must likewise proclaim it with urgency and faithfulness because it is, quite simply, a matter of life and death for his hearers. If he loses sight of the coming appearance of Jesus he will lose his sense of urgency and his cutting edge.

The solemn charge that Paul has been building toward is simple in its expression but far-reaching in its implications: **'Preach the word'** (4:2). Notice that in this brief instruction Paul specifies both the nature of the activity and the substance of the proclamation. The substance of Timothy's ministry is to be the word of God – the Scriptural word that Paul has been speaking of in previous verses. Timothy is to continue in faithfulness to the biblical and apostolic gospel (3:14) by preaching the word and nothing but the word. How easy it is to become frightened of preaching what the word actually says and so hold back from speaking the truth in its fullness. How easy it is to become discouraged from a lack of fruit in word ministry and so turn to another subject and another message. Timothy is to proclaim the word and nothing else.

The nature of his activity is to 'preach'. The Greek verb *kēryssein* means to 'proclaim' or 'declare'. The implication is that Timothy (as one set apart to be God's spokesman, 'the man of God', 3:17) is to deliver the message of the word with authority and urgency. This is no mere impartation of information; it is an authoritative declaration of God's word. Because Timothy is bound to say only what the word of God says – he is delivering God's message and not his own – he can have the confidence to proclaim it in this way.

Now follow a number of instructions that support the central charge to 'preach the word' and show the manner in which Timothy is to carry it out.[2] Timothy must '**be prepared in season and out of season**' (4:2). Paul does not specify whose 'season' he has in mind. He could mean the 'season' in which Timothy finds himself. He is to preach when he feels inclined to preach and finds it convenient to preach, and he is to preach when he is discouraged in his ministry and the thought of Sunday fills him with dread. Alternatively, Paul could refer to the season in which the church finds itself. Timothy is to preach whether or not the people feel inclined and prepared to listen to Bible teaching. Or he could have in mind the 'season' of society at large. Timothy is to preach when the community is in an age of openness and receptivity, and when it is in an age of unhearing hostility to the gospel. Probably all three types of 'season' fall within the scope of Paul's interest and concern here. The implication is this: Timothy is to commit himself to the proclamation of God's word whether he feels like it or

---

2   Formally it is possible that verse 2 provides a list of separate and distinct instructions (preach the word, be prepared, correct, rebuke and encourage) with only the final two elements of the list showing the manner in which the list of instructions (or perhaps even just the final instruction) should be carried out. This is possible, but the central importance that Paul assigns to the charge to 'preach the word' by placing it at the front of the list and directly after the solemn preface to the charge suggests that this instruction is indeed the central instruction, and is supported by the instructions that follow in verse 2. More than that, the charge to 'be ready in season and out of season' is not an instruction that can stand alone. On its own it would beg the question, 'Be ready to do what....?' The answer must be, 'To preach the Word'. Given that this second instruction supports and modifies the central instruction to 'preach the word', it seems right to take the rest of the instructions of the verse as functioning in the same way. All that having been said, the final two elements of the list are not verbs but nouns that identify characteristics that are to mark the proclamation, so there is some distinction here. It would be possible to amplify the meaning of 4:2 with the following paraphrase: 'Preach the word; be prepared to do this in season and out of season; in your preaching ministry, correct, rebuke and encourage, and do so with patience and careful instruction.'

not, whether the church family are listening and hungry or not, and whether the society at large is receptive or hostile. In season and out of season, Timothy is to preach the word.

Paul reminds Timothy that his preaching of the word should involve three vital elements. He is to '**correct, rebuke and encourage**' (4:2). Timothy must use the word as it is designed to be used (see 3:16) to correct wrong doctrine with true doctrine and rebuke wrong behaviour. The dangerous situation currently at Ephesus (2:16-18) and on the horizon for the future (3:1-9) means that these aspects of Timothy's preaching ministry will be of vital importance for the protection of the church. Paul takes the trouble to remind Timothy of the need to include correcting and rebuking in his preaching ministry because it would be all too easy for him to leave out those elements. It is, after all, personally uncomfortable to correct and rebuke others. It will not make Timothy popular. But the Bible gives him both the authority and the means of carrying out this vital aspect of his task.

Just as it would be easy in some circumstances for a preacher to neglect to correct or rebuke the people under his care, so too he could fail to '**encourage**' (preachers will probably be naturally disposed toward either correction or encouragement and need to aim for faithful balance). The biblical language of 'encouragement' carries not only the nuance of comfort but also of urging and exhortation. Once he has corrected wrong belief and action, the preacher must then positively spur the people on to rightly embrace true gospel doctrine and living. And where he sees the gospel bearing fruit in the lives of the people he ministers to, the preacher needs to encourage them by marking the fact that the Spirit is indeed at work in them (as Paul often did in his ministry; see, for example, 1 Thess. 1:2-10).

Finally, the multifaceted task of preaching the word must be done **'with great patience and careful instruction'.** Timothy will need to remember that it takes time to learn the truth. He will need to repeat himself and return to the same truths and the same passages of Scripture again and again. There will be some in the church family who are especially slow to learn or reluctant to learn. Timothy will need to be patient with them, and perhaps spend time with them one-to-one as well. His patient proclamation must always be grounded in careful teaching of what Scripture says. Preaching is more than teaching; as we have seen already, it is an authoritative declaration of the truth. Simply reducing the preaching of the word of God to 'teaching the Bible' (as we so often do) is to minimise and domesticate preaching. But it is vital to see that preaching is *never less* than teaching and is always grounded in careful explanation of what the text says and how it applies. As Martyn Lloyd-Jones famously described it, preaching is 'logic on fire'.[3] The fire is wonderful; where there is no fire, the declaration of God's truth feels limp and lacks its rightful authoritative conviction. But we must not allow logic to disappear in a blaze of glory, and so Paul reminds Timothy to preach 'with careful instruction'.

Paul does not issue these instructions in a vacuum. He sees the urgent necessity of reminding Timothy of his task and how to go about it because he knows that there will be hard times ahead. If you like, he can see that Bible preaching will be very much 'out of season' before too long. **'For the time**

3   Lloyd-Jones, D. M., *Preaching and Preachers*, Second edition, (London, U.K.: Hodder and Stoughton, 1985), p. 97.

will come when men will not put up with sound doctrine. Instead, to suit their own desires they will gather around them a great number of teachers to say what their itching ears want to hear. They will turn their ears away from the truth and turn aside to myths' (4:3-4). Timothy should not expect that a divine mandate to preach or a God-breathed word to deliver will guarantee a positive reception. Paul the apostle has met with frequent rejection and now writes to Timothy from a prison cell, abandoned by his friends. Timothy must faithfully and doggedly stick to his task, but he must be prepared for rejection. 'Sound doctrine' – the doctrine centred on a Christ who died before he rose and who calls his followers to walk in his way (2:8-13) – is not naturally appealing to the sinful human heart. It is particularly unappealing when it is delivered with correction and rebuke (4:2). Timothy should expect that 'the time will come' when people simply will not 'put up' with it. They will prefer false teachers who peddle an easier gospel (2:18) and who confirm them in their love of self, money and pleasure (3:1-5). Even as Timothy proclaims the 'truth', they will defiantly 'turn their ears away' from it and embrace 'myths'.

When such seasons come, even if all around him are rejecting the truth, Timothy is to stand out from the crowd and just keep going. Paul turns the spotlight now on Timothy as a person and his own character, and he calls him to adopt a set of dispositions and behaviours that will enable him to maintain a faithful ministry through all the ups and downs that certainly lie before him. '**But you, keep your head in all situations**' (4:5). As before (2:1, 3:10, 3:14), Timothy is to be boldly counter-cultural. He is to be 'sober' (the literal rendering of 'keep your head') and unmoved in his commitment to the truth and to the hard work of proclaiming it. When the false teachers that people gather around them proclaim a new and easier gospel, Timothy is to 'continue' (3:14) in the true gospel. When false teachers draw crowds with novel doctrines, Timothy is to content himself with a sometimes frosty and meagre reception when he proclaims biblical doctrine. 'When men and women get intoxicated with heady heresies and sparkling novelties, ministers must keep "calm and sane" (NEB).'[4]

This will undoubtedly make life difficult for Timothy as it did for Paul, and so it is no surprise that in this context Paul calls Timothy again (see 1:8, 2:3) to **'endure hardship'**. There will be a constant temptation for Timothy simply to give up for the sake of a quiet life, but he must follow Paul's example (4:6-8) and endure. More than that, as friends and trusted allies turn against him and his message, there will be tremendous pressure for Timothy to spend all his time firefighting and managing crises – and he could easily neglect the work of proclaiming the gospel to those who will listen. So Paul reminds him that he must always **'do the work of an evangelist'**. We are still within the orbit of the central charge of 4:2 to 'preach the word', so, on the primary level, Paul charges Timothy here to keep preaching the gospel and not simply to spend all his time responding to error. But this charge extends beyond formal preaching as well; Timothy must invest himself in the work of spreading the good news as a personal evangelist.[5]

---

4   Stott, *Message*, p. 112.

5   We might be tempted to limit the scope of this charge as applying only to Timothy (and not to pastor-teachers more generally), imagining that Timothy had a particular gift for evangelism that made the charge uniquely relevant to him. However, there is little evidence that Timothy was uniquely or unusually gifted in this regard, and in any case, this charge comes to him as a representative leader and teacher of God's people (a 'man of God', 3:17). It should be taken as establishing an authoritative pattern for pastor-teachers to follow.

Finally, as his last general instruction for the future of his ministry, Paul instructs Timothy to **'discharge all the duties of [or, 'fulfil'] your ministry'** (4:5). Timothy must, quite simply, keep going and not give up. He must finish the job that God has given him to do even if he is opposed for doing it, even if he is abandoned by his friends, even if he sees little fruit. He must carry on. In the following verses Paul will remind Timothy that he himself has done just that. Paul knows that the overwhelming barrier to long-term faithfulness in ministry is sheer discouragement. He knows that the way that the devil would love to derail the effectiveness of Timothy's work is simply to convince him to quit. And he knows that any gospel minister who stays the course is nothing short of a miracle of God's grace. So his final call is simply to keep going until the work is finished. In an age when the statisticians tell us that the drop-off rate for ministers is startlingly high, Paul's charge is as urgent as ever.

From text to message

Theme and aim

Theme:	Pastor-teachers must faithfully proclaim the word, in light of judgment, whatever the response.
Aim (for the pastor-teacher):	Preach the word.
Aim (for the church):	Seek and prayerfully support ministers who will preach the word; receive the word gladly.

A way in

We might begin by focusing on the priority of word ministry in the local church: 'In some churches and denominations, when it comes time to seek out a new minister, the church family will be invited to fill out a survey intended to discover what they want most in a new minister. Sometimes the church family will be invited to list key skills in a ranking order of priority. These might include organisational ability, commitment to home visits, aptitude for making new links in the community, ability to relate to children and young people, ability in teaching and preaching the Bible, and any number of other things. There should be no doubt in any of our minds which skill should always rank as number one. If there is any doubt, Paul sets out to clarify in our minds what must be central and remain central in the ministry of any pastor-teacher: he must "preach the word."'

Alternatively, a preacher who is speaking to a group of ministers or who is preaching to a congregation in which many people are active in some form of word ministry might focus on the motivation to endure in word ministry: 'Word ministry is hard work. It takes labour to understand the text clearly; it takes patience to teach and re-teach it; it takes endurance to do so in the face of apathy and opposition. What will keep you and me going in our various forms of word-ministry, for the long run? Paul, for his part, has reached the end of his ministry and he has kept at it, and so it should not surprise us if he has something to teach us in this. And, sure enough, his charge to young Timothy to keep going with the proclamation of the word gives us one key truth to keep in view and that will certainly motivate us to keep going. The key truth is this: Jesus the Judge will return.'

Ideas for application

+ Look for Bible teachers whose preaching reflects the sober awareness of the coming judgment and who are unafraid to speak about it.

+ As a Bible teacher, reflect often on the fact that you will have to give an account for your ministry, and remember that your job is to prepare your hearers to meet Jesus when he returns as King and Judge.

+ Look for preachers who are committed to preaching the word *and the word only*. If you are a Bible teacher, have that commitment yourself.

+ Look for Bible teachers who will faithfully and boldly preach the word *whatever the season* of their own lives, of the church family, and of society at large. If you are a gospel minister, commit yourself to doing just that.

+ Look for Bible teachers who will correct, rebuke and encourage – and not neglect any of those vital aspects of biblical ministry. If you are a Bible teacher, ensure that each of those three elements is constantly present in your teaching and preaching.

+ Look for Bible teachers who are patient in their instruction and who take the trouble to teach the word carefully.

+ If you are a Bible teacher, ensure that you are being patient and instructing the people under your care. Do you need to work harder at simplifying, illustrating and applying your teaching? Are there practical steps you can take to make your preaching more accessible and easier to listen to? Do you need to give times over to question and answer sessions? Could you be more available for one-to-one ministry with people who are particularly hungry to learn?

* Take warning that there will be times when some professing Christians will refuse to accept the truth and will seek false teachers. If you are a Bible teacher, do not be shocked; if you are a church member, pray that you will not be such a one.

* Look for Bible teachers who have the ballast and emotional stability to keep their head in times of crisis and pressure. It is not enough for someone to be a capable teacher; personal stability is vital in a gospel minister.

* Gospel ministers must be prepared to endure hardship; church families must pray for and support them.

* Look for gospel ministers who are committed to evangelism, especially (but not only) in their preaching. If you are a preacher, ensure that the gospel message is regularly made clear to the unbeliever from your preaching, and ensure that you are prayerfully committed to personal evangelism as God gives you opportunities.

* Gospel ministers must pray for God's help to persevere in the ministry God has given them to do. This does not mean never moving from one ministry post to another (sometimes it will be wise and right to move), but it does mean that a Gospel minister's disposition should be to stay until a job is finished rather than to leave as soon as things become wearisome or difficult.

* In light of all these lessons, pray for your ministers!

Suggestions for preaching

Paul calls Timothy to a ministry of biblical faithfulness (see 3:14-17) that will endure as his ministry has endured (see 4:6-8). These verses are the central verses of the letter and constitute a manifesto for a ministry that is faithful and endures. It could be divided as follows:

1. The crucial outlook for the gospel preacher (4:1)

2. The central task of the gospel preacher (4:2)

3. The coming challenges for the gospel preacher (4:3-4)

4. The character needed in the gospel preacher (4:5)

Suggestions for teaching

Questions to help understand the text

1. What does Paul mean by Jesus' 'appearing' and 'kingdom' (4:1)? Why does he mention them here? Why does he mention the judgment?

2. What is the charge given to Timothy (4:2)? How is he to carry it out?

3. Paul expands on the basic instruction to 'preach the word' with six supplementary instructions. What do each of these add? Or, to put it another way, how would Timothy's ministry be weakened if he neglected any one of them?

4. How does the charge of verses 1-2 build upon the previous verses, 3:14-17?

5. What is the warning of verses 3-4? Why does Paul issue it here?

6. In the face of opposition, how should Timothy respond (4:5)? Why is this the right way to respond?

Questions to help apply the text

1. To what extent do I prize the teaching of the word? What do I look for in a minister and in a church? Where does the preaching of the word feature in my criteria? How do I encourage my minister in his preaching of the word, and do I pray for him in that task?

2. Do I carry out my own Bible teaching in light of the coming of Jesus? How would my Bible teaching change if I prompted myself constantly to remember that I will have to give an account for my faithfulness in it and that my hearers can only be ready for that day through the faithful preaching and teaching of the word?

3. What are the seasons in the life of the minister, the church family and the society at large that may affect the proclamation and reception of the word? If you are a minister, what season are you in personally? What season is your church in? What season is society in?

4. And so, what are the particular challenges facing preachers of the word where you are?

5. To what extent are verses 3-4 true in your context today? What is the right response, in your context, to the sober warning of these verses?

6. If you are a pastor-teacher, what should be your prayerful priorities for personal growth in light of verse 5?

7. How do these verses shape your vision of a faithful ministry (and so choose what kind of church to be part of and what kind of leaders to follow)?

8. How do these verses help you to pray for your ministers? What are two or three specific things you can be praying regularly for your ministers in light of this passage?

8

A PATTERN OF FAITHFULNESS
(4:6-8)

For I am already being poured out like a drink offering, and the time has come for my departure. I have fought the good fight, I have finished the race, I have kept the faith. Now there is in store for me the crown of righteousness, which the Lord, the righteous Judge, will award to me on that day – and not only to me, but also to all who have longed for his appearing.

Introduction

In this short section Paul returns to his own model to provide an example of the kind of faithful persevering ministry that he has just called Timothy to commit himself to. He moves beyond his ministry history and his present expectation of death to his great confidence for the future – a confidence that Timothy and the whole church may share.

Listening to the text

Context and structure

These verses are linked closely to the preceding section both logically and formally, beginning as they do with the logical connector, 'For I....' (4:6). As he sets out his personal model for Timothy to emulate, Paul begins by outlining his present condition (4:6-7), then surveys his ministry history, and finishes by sharing his firm confidence for the future (4:8). In the following verses Paul will move from this big-picture overview of his ministry model to share news of his ministry associates and to consider a number of practicalities. Verses 8 and 9 will be linked to a certain extent by the overlapping theme of 'love'.

Working through the text

As he does frequently throughout the letter, Paul offers his own personal example to illustrate and reinforce the lessons he has been teaching Timothy. Verse 6 follows on naturally from the logical flow of the preceding verses. Paul has shown how the ungodly will behave in rejecting the truth (4:3-4). Against the backdrop of their behaviour, Timothy must stand out (*'But you....'*, 4:5). Paul now provides the basis for his instruction for Timothy to stand apart – his own personal model (*'For I....'*, 4:6). There is, then, a logical progression (to paraphrase): *they* will act in faithlessness; *but you* must endure; *for I* have set a model of faithful endurance.

Paul begins by focusing on his present situation: **'For I am already being poured out like a drink offering'** (4:6). The 'drink offering' was an offering of wine or oil poured out as a main offering or as an accompaniment to another offering (Exod. 29:40-41; Lev. 23:12-13; Num. 15:5-10,

15:22-24, 28:7-8; see Phil. 2:17). It accompanied the animal sacrifice in various contexts, including the daily offering. As a drink offering went alongside and complemented the animal sacrifice, so Paul's offering of himself and giving of his life for the gospel complements the definitive sacrifice of Jesus.[1] The work of Christ was complete, but through Paul's self-sacrifice the effect of his work is spread as the gospel goes out. Green's comments here are helpful: 'being *poured out* is Paul's explanation of how it is that his experience of suffering goes hand-in-hand with people hearing about Jesus. The growth of the church is costly for him – much as a drink offering would be – because throwing away the best wine was an apparent waste of good money, and keeping Paul in prison was a waste of a good apostle. But Paul was willing to pay that price if the result was conversions.'[2] That Paul can say that he is 'already being poured out' indicates that the process leading to his death has already begun.

Should we be in any doubt what Paul is implying here, he reinforces the point by affirming that **'the time has come for my departure'** (4:6). The term **'departure'** (Gk. *analysis*), which literally means 'loosing', points to Paul's impending death. It could envision Paul's departure as the loosing of his chains, perhaps to be led off for execution, or the loosing of ropes to set a ship free to cast off (a rather more romantic image!). In any case, the implication is clear: Paul expects

---

1   In Philippians 2:17 Paul uses similar imagery, but there the sacrifice is explicitly named as the 'sacrifice and service coming from your faith'. Here in 2 Timothy 4:6 there is no indication that the sacrifice of Timothy's faith (or that of any other believer) is in view, so it would seem most likely that the primary and ultimate sacrifice – the sacrifice of Jesus – is in view.

2   Green, C., *Finishing the race: reading 2 Timothy today* (Sydney, Australia: Aquila Press, 2000), pp. 143-44.

to die soon (see his use of similar language with a clear reference to death in Philippians 1:23).

This stark assessment of Paul's present situation serves largely as a model for Timothy. Paul has been faithful to the end, and he calls Timothy to the same faithfulness. But there is, in all likelihood, an additional layer to the logical connection between 4:6 and what came before (indicated by the 'For....' that links verse 6 to the preceding verses): the fact that Paul expects to die soon *adds urgency* to the instructions of 4:1-5. Timothy must preach the word faithfully and endure hard times because Paul is more or less finished. The future of gospel ministry now rests on the shoulders of young leaders like Timothy.

Now follow three different retrospective summaries of Paul's life and ministry: **'I have fought the good fight, I have finished the race, I have kept the faith'** (4:7). The two images of a fight and a race remind us of the toil, struggle and (sometimes) sheer pain involved in Christian life and ministry for Paul. He has proved through his own experience that 'everyone who wants to live a godly life in Christ Jesus will be persecuted' (3:12), and he has shown through his own ministry that suffering and hardship are simply part of the job (1:8, 2:3, 4:5). These two images of physical struggle point ultimately to Paul's settled and costly allegiance to the Lord Jesus and his gospel. In fighting and running to the end, he can justly claim that he has 'finished the race'. And it is to this same faithfulness that he now calls Timothy.

Paul has already taught us that in God's economy suffering precedes glory (2:8-11), and so, having reminded us of his own suffering, he now joyfully points us to the glory awaiting him: **'Now there is in store for me the crown of** righteousness, which the Lord, the righteous Judge, will award to me on that day...' (4:8a). Paul has not abandoned his athletic metaphor; the crown here recalls the wreath crown that victors in an ancient athletic contest would wear. The precise significance of the 'crown of righteousness' requires some careful consideration. It seems unlikely that it simply refers to the gift of righteousness because Paul teaches elsewhere that believers have already been justified and so made righteous (Rom. 5:1). It seems more likely that Paul is envisioning a final declaration and confirmation of the righteousness he has already received. When he stands before the Lord on that final day, he will enter fully into his salvation and be conformed in every respect to the character of righteousness which he already possessed by faith. The term translated 'righteousness' here is of the same family as the verb 'justify'; it simply means one who is justified. Stott notes that Paul's choice of this term here stands 'in deliberate contrast to the sentence he is expecting any day to receive from a human judge in a human court. The Emperor Nero may declare him guilty and condemn him to death, but there will soon come a "magnificent reversal of Nero's verdict" when "the Lord, the righteous judge", declares him righteous.'[3]

This promised 'crown of righteousness' is not only for Paul but for 'all who have longed for [lit., 'loved'] his appearing'. The theme of love has featured prominently in chapter 3. The terrible people of terrible times will be marked by a lack of love for God and all that is good, and instead will be consumed by love for self, money and pleasure (3:1-5). As we shall see in the next verses, the

---

3   Stott, *Message*, p. 115, quoting Simpson, E.K., *The Pastoral Epistles: The Greek text* (London, UK: Tyndale Press, 1954).

problem with Paul's former ministry associate Demas, and the reason why he abandoned Paul, was that 'he loved this world' (4:10). Those who 'have loved' the appearing of the Lord Jesus are those whose hearts are filled with longing for his return and whose sights are firmly set on that day. Because their hearts are consumed with longing for the return of Christ, the competing loves of self, money and pleasure are not allowed to dominate their affections or drive their concerns. Those who love this way and live this way are those who truly believe the gospel of life – and so they are those who will enter into that promised life at the final day. Here again we see Paul writing to Timothy, but with clear regard for the whole church family who will be listening in. The implication is clear: they too may share his confidence if they too will keep their hearts set on the appearing of Jesus.

From text to message

Theme and aim

Theme:	Paul models faithful ministry and confident future expectation.
Aim:	Follow Paul's model of faithfulness; love Jesus' appearing.

A way in

The preacher might use Paul's image of Christian life and ministry as a race (see 4:7) and begin: 'In the prime of his athletic career, the British track and field champion Mo Farah collapsed at the finish line of a half-marathon in New York and had to be taken away in a wheelchair. For such a superb athlete, it was worrying to see his strength give way. However, he brushed off concerns for his health and explained that there was a simple reason for the collapse: "I tried so hard in the race". He had a goal in mind, and he literally gave it his all.'

'Serving the Lord Jesus in any form of gospel ministry is hard work. Whenever we minister to others with the aim that they should trust Jesus and become more like him, the work will be both relentless and limitless, and there will always be opposition. What will keep us going in our particular ministry for the long haul and when the going gets tough? As Paul approaches the end of his life and ministry – his "race", as he calls it – he shows us that he has the ultimate goal in mind. In these verses Paul shares with us the outlook on the future that will fuel faithful, persevering ministry in the present.'

Ideas for application

+ Paul sees his life as a sacrifice poured out to the Lord for the sake of the church. How would the character of our ministry and service change if we saw our own lives in that way?

+ It is a good ambition for any gospel minister and any Christian to be able to say at the end of his or her life, 'I have fought the good fight, I have finished the race, I have kept the faith.' How can we live and minister *now*, in order to enable us to say those words *then*?

+ It is sobering to consider the inverse, that we might reach the end of our lives and be unable to say with integrity that we have fought and run well.

- It is important to remember the gospel when considering this life review; every believer (Paul included!) would be conscious of sin and failure when looking back. Paul's contented perspective on the past is not a claim to sinless perfection, but is nonetheless a recognition that he remained committed to the Lord Jesus and the gospel. Ultimately, a contented perspective on the past is only possible because of the blood of Jesus, which covers the many sins and failures of the past (some will feel instantly convicted and defeated when they read verse 7 and consider their own failures, so make a point of preaching and teaching the gospel of grace here!).

- Paul was only able to live and minister as he did because he lived constantly in light of the judgment and in confident hope of his final salvation. We too must have our appearance before the righteous Judge constantly in view if we are to endure in faithfulness.

- Ultimate salvation is only for those whose hearts are set on the appearing of Jesus. Do we long for his appearing, or are the affections of our hearts fixed elsewhere?

Suggestions for preaching

Paul's personal model of faithfulness in life and ministry is the focus here. He shows us how to finish well as a servant of the Lord Jesus – modelling a contented and confident perspective on both the past and the future. This insight into Paul's retrospective view of his life and ministry and his confident and believing hope for the future is given so that Timothy and all believers might strive to end life with the same confident outlook. For preaching, it would seem most straightforward to divide the passage up in two parts, considering first Paul's retrospect and then his prospect:

The faithful gospel servant – how to finish well.

1. Looking back in contentment (4:6-7)

2. Looking forward in hope (4:8)

Suggestions for teaching

Questions to help understand the text

1. Read Numbers 15:5-10 and 15:22-24. What is the image Paul is using here in 2 Timothy 4:6? What is the primary sacrifice he has in mind? How does the 'pouring out' of his life as a drink offering complement the main sacrifice?

2. How does Paul feel as he looks back on his life (4:7)? Why? Does he imply that he has lived and ministered perfectly?

3. Paul cannot mean in 4:8 that he will be given the gift of righteousness, because he teaches elsewhere that he has already received that gift (see Rom. 5:1-2). What is the 'crown of righteousness' that he looks forward to receiving?

4. Why, from 2 Timothy, can Paul expect the 'righteous Judge' to award to him, as sinner, the 'crown of righteousness' (4:8)?

5. From 4:8, how can Paul and others be confident of receiving the crown?

6. The term sometimes translated 'longed for' is literally 'loved'. Read again 3:1-5. How is the love of 4:8 unlike the warped loves described in those verses (note also the warped love of 4:10)? Why is the 'love' of 4:8 ultimately tied to salvation?

Questions to help apply the text

1. Could you describe your life and service of the Lord Jesus and his church using the image of 4:6a? How are you challenged by that imagery?

2. What in your life and ministry now would hinder you from making the declaration of 4:7 at the end of your life? If you set the words of 4:7 as your goal – that you would be able to say them at the end – how will things need to change in your life now?

3. How does 4:7 shape our prayers for each other and for ourselves?

4. What will the life and ministry of a pastor look like who is 'fighting' and 'running' well? What will it look like if he has stopped doing so? How should this verse shape our prayers for our church leaders?

5. Do we love and long for the return of Jesus more than we love ourselves and the things of this world? What will be the signs that we love ourselves and this world? What will be the signs that we love his appearing?

6. How does the prospect of the 'crown of righteousness' motivate and encourage our service of the Lord Jesus and his people?

9

THE FAITHFUL GOSPEL STRATEGIST
(4:9-22)

Do your best to come to me quickly, for Demas, because he loved this world, has deserted me and has gone to Thessalonica. Crescens has gone to Galatia, and Titus to Dalmatia. Only Luke is with me. Get Mark and bring him with you, because he is helpful to me in my ministry. I sent Tychicus to Ephesus. When you come, bring the cloak that I left with Carpus at Troas, and my scrolls, especially the parchments.

Alexander the metalworker did me a great deal of harm. The Lord will repay him for what he has done. You too should be on your guard against him, because he strongly opposed our message.

At my first defence, no-one came to my support, but everyone deserted me. May it not be held against them. But the Lord stood at my side and gave me strength, so that through me the message might be fully proclaimed and all the Gentiles might hear it. And I was delivered from the lion's mouth. The Lord will rescue me from every evil attack and will bring me safely to his heavenly kingdom. To him be glory for ever and ever. Amen.

Greet Priscilla and Aquila and the household of Onesiphorus. Erastus stayed in Corinth, and I left Trophimus sick in Miletus. Do your best to get here before winter. Eubulus greets you, and so do Pudens, Linus, Claudia and all the brothers.

The Lord be with your spirit. Grace be with you.

Introduction

This extended section of final personal instructions and greetings is easily overlooked as being of secondary importance. But Paul has insisted earlier in this very letter that 'all Scripture is God-breathed and is useful...' for equipping 'the man of God' for ministry (3:16-17). Paul's insistence on the usefulness of all Scripture applies to these verses here, and we overlook them to our loss. As so often in the letter, Paul is offering to Timothy and to us a window into his own model of ministry that we might learn from it and emulate it. In particular, Paul here gives us a vital insight into how he views and seeks to deploy his 'team' of ministry associates in a strategic way for the work of the gospel.

Listening to the text

Context and structure

In the previous verses Paul has made it clear that he believes he is now at the end of his life and ministry. However, although death is imminent, Paul does not know the precise timing of his death, and so he proceeds now to issue a set of final instructions to Timothy regarding practical arrangements.

These practical arrangements include mention of various things that Paul needs (clothes, books), but they focus primarily on liaising with Paul's broader network of ministry partners. These verses are linked to the previous verses partly through the presence of the verb 'love' in verse 10 (see 4:8 and comments on that verse), which acts as something of a bridge between the two paragraphs, tying Paul's reflections on his own ministry and his future hope to the tragedy of Demas' desertion. In the middle of these practical instructions Paul recalls his trial and expresses his gratitude for God's deliverance and his continued trust in God's protection. He ends the section and the letter with a final blessing.

Working through the text
Paul now moves from the broader picture of his life and ministry as viewed in light of the appearing of Jesus and focuses in on the current practical details of his situation. He is isolated in prison in Rome, and he longs for Timothy to join him and provide support to him (4:9). Perhaps the most tragic cause of Paul's isolation is the desertion of Demas, a former close ministry associate (his name is coupled with Luke's at Col. 4:14 and Philem. 24), who has abandoned Paul **'because he loved this world'** (4:10). Demas stands in direct contrast to Paul and all faithful believers who have (lit.) 'loved his [Christ's] appearing' and who stand to inherit the 'crown of righteousness' (4:8). The issue of misdirected love is a significant sub-theme of the letter. Remember that the people of the terrible times (3:1-5) will be people with misdirected love. Rather than loving God and all that is good, they will instead be lovers of themselves, money and pleasure. Paul's fears for the church in Ephesus are clearly well grounded. Some years later, the Lord has this message for the church in Ephesus:

'Yet I hold this against you: You have forsaken your first love' (Rev. 2:4).

Demas, for his part, has set his love not on Jesus and his appearing but on this present world. There is a resonance here with the heresy of Hymenaeus and Philetus, who propagate the error that the resurrection of the people of God has already happened (2:18), implying that believers should expect to live the good life in the here and now. When faced with the choice between casting in his lot with a suffering and imprisoned apostle and cutting loose and finding a quiet life elsewhere, Demas chose the latter.

A number of commentators have made the sobering observation that there is no indication here that Demas formally renounced his faith or even quit Christian ministry. All we know is that he moved off to Thessalonica, perhaps to carry out a different ministry there. He may have seen that there was less hostility and a warmer reception for him and his message in Thessalonica, so he simply went where he thought things would be less challenging. It is easy for us to pour scorn on Demas and shake our heads at his sorry tale. The less comfortable reality to consider is just how readily any of us could do the same as he did, but for the grace of God.

In the Greek, the desertion of Demas is followed without pause and in the same grammatical unit by mention of the departure of Crescens and Titus (4:10). It is not impossible that the implication is that they have deserted Paul too;[1] however it seems probable that if such a key figure as Titus had defected, there would be more comment. More likely, these other two associates have gone on for legitimate

---

1   Green, *Finishing*, p. 149.

reasons tied to their assigned ministries, but mention of their departure highlights again Paul's isolation.

As this overview of people movement progresses it becomes clear that Paul's central concern here is not his personal isolation, but ultimately the progress of the gospel and the health of the church around the Mediterranean rim. Paul charges Timothy to **'Get Mark and bring him with you, because he is helpful to me in my ministry'** (4:11). Mark must come to Rome because Paul needs him for the work of the Gospel there. Given what we have learned about Demas' desertion of Paul, it is striking to remember that Paul once deemed Mark unfit to join him on his missionary journeys because he had formerly been a deserter (Acts 15:38).[2] Mark's evident restoration to friendship with Paul and to ministry alongside the apostle (see also Col. 4:10, Philem. 24) gives a glimmer of hope to those who read this section of 2 Timothy with a heavy heart, feeling that they may have let fellow gospel workers down at some stage. Timothy is also of vital importance to Paul; apart from anything else, Paul needs him to bring his scrolls and parchments to aid him in his study (4:13). But in summoning Timothy to Rome, Paul has not forgotten the church in Ephesus with all its spiritual needs: **'I sent Tychicus to Ephesus'** (4:12). Paul had previously contemplated sending Tychicus to Crete to replace Titus, but has presumably sent Artemas instead (see Titus 3:12).

We may naturally hold in our minds the picture of Paul the lone ranger, charging around the Mediterranean more

---

2   Although Mark was a relatively common name, there is no reason to assume that Paul is speaking of a different Mark here. Had he wished to refer to another Mark it seems reasonable to assume that he would have made this clear by adding another element of identification.

or less in isolation, blazing an independent trail for the gospel. But the reality is rather different; Paul was a team player. It is clear from his instruction to Timothy in 2:2 to raise up future leaders that Paul had a vision for doing just that in his own ministry. If we add up the number of names of Paul's ministry associates mentioned in his letters and Acts we find that there were about 100 people alongside whom Paul was labouring for the gospel.[3] This final section of 2 Timothy is a vivid reminder that Paul was a team player (vv. 19-21 particularly reinforce the point). More than that, it provides for us a window into his strategic thinking. Paul had in his mind a map of the Mediterranean world, and he was constantly thinking about who was needed where to further the cause of the gospel. As in so many other respects, Paul here provides a model for ministry. He invests in people who can be gospel workers, and then thinks strategically about their deployment and re-deployment.

In verse 13 Paul gives us another window into his personal model of ministry and his outlook on his final days: **'When you come, bring the cloak that I left with Carpus at Troas, and my scrolls, especially the parchments.'** Paul believes firmly that his death at the hands of the Roman authorities is imminent (4:6), but he does not know the precise timing of his execution. So, he continues to think in practical terms: he needs his cloak in order to stay warm as winter approaches (see 4:21a), and he needs his scrolls to continue his study. The second request is particularly instructive. We do not know precisely what these scrolls and parchments contained, but it seems most likely on balance that they were Scripture texts, possibly alongside commentaries and

3   See Earle Ellis, E. 'Paul and his co-workers,' *New Testament Studies* 17 (1971), pp. 437-52.

Paul's own notes. Paul was a learned man who had been well trained in the Scriptures, and we see his grasp of theological truth writ large in his letters and in his preaching ministry as recorded in Acts. But even for such a great theologian and Bible teacher as Paul, his dying wish was to be able to study more and to deepen his knowledge of the Scriptures. In remaining an avid student of the word until the end, Paul sets a pattern for other gospel ministers to follow.

While this section resounds with the joy and buzz of gospel partnership with a wide network of people, it also reflects the tragic experience of defection, opposition and even isolation. We have seen that experience already in the story of Demas (4:10), and the issue re-surfaces in verse 14 with mention of **Alexander the metalworker**. Alexander was introduced in 1 Timothy 1:19 as someone who has 'rejected' 'faith and a good conscience' and so 'shipwrecked' his faith. Paul has taken steps to discipline him and to exclude him from the fellowship of believers (1 Tim. 1:20), but that has not stopped Alexander opposing the message or doing Paul and his ministry a great deal of harm (2 Tim. 4:14). Timothy must be on guard against him (4:15).

Alexander is not the only former friend who has disappointed Paul; others have let him down in perhaps less dramatic ways, but the result was that 'At my first defence, no-one came to my support, but everyone deserted me'. (4:16). All this has undoubtedly brought sadness to Paul, but he recounts this experience, not to discourage Timothy (although it will certainly sober him), but rather to encourage him. Alexander may have opposed Paul and may be a danger to Timothy, but the Lord is still in control of the situation: 'The Lord will repay him for what he has done' (4:14b). Paul may have been abandoned at his trial at Rome, with no one to speak up for him, **'But the Lord stood at my side and gave me strength.'** Indeed, the Lord brought him through that experience so that the Lord, through Paul, might continue to proclaim the Gospel in Rome (**'...so that through me the message might be fully proclaimed....'** 4:17a), perhaps even on the occasion of the trial itself (4:17a). It may be that Paul was facing the threat of quite literally being thrown to the lions by the Romans (4:17b), but the Lord saved him from that. In fact, Paul is confident that nothing can overwhelm God and his plans for him: **'The Lord will rescue me from every evil attack and will bring me safely to his heavenly kingdom'** (4:18).

Paul's purpose in recounting his trials is not to garner pity or to seek congratulation for his steadfastness, but to point Timothy and the listening church to God's power and faithfulness, that they might take heart and remain resolute in his service. Because God has been the primary mover in Paul's ministry and because he has achieved what he set out to achieve in and through that ministry, Paul calls Timothy and all who read his words to give God, and not Paul, the glory: **'To him be glory for ever and ever. Amen'** (4:18).

Paul could be forgiven for concluding his final letter – sent from prison, with the prospect of death looming – on a note of self-pity. But there is none of that in the final verses. Instead, Paul finishes in his characteristic way with concern for, and interest in, his friends and gospel partners. He sends greetings, gives a brief report on the movements of fellow workers and adds the request that Timothy make his way to Rome before winter weather hinders his journey (4:19-21). For Paul, gospel ministry can never be separated from a concern for people and is always carried out in the context of a rich network of personal relationships. He concludes with a blessing, praying that the Lord would be with Timothy's spirit, and that 'grace' would be with 'you' (4:22).

As noted already, the final 'you' is plural. Paul expects this letter to be read publicly, and he prays for God's grace (which has featured before in this letter; see 1:2, 1:9, 2:1) to be with the whole church family at Ephesus. This brief window into Paul's expected wider audience for this letter reminds us that it is a letter *to* Timothy, but *for* the whole church.

From text to message

Theme and aim

Theme:	Under God's sovereignty, strategic partnerships are key to enabling gospel ministry.
Aim:	Trusting God's sovereignty, rejoice in and invest in gospel partnerships.

A way in

We might begin by addressing the perceived unimportance of the closing sections of Paul's letters: 'If you are anything like me, you will be tempted to skim over the final verses of Paul's letters. His sharing news about his friends and sending greetings to various people is a nice touch, but essentially window-dressing, we assume. We are pretty sure that these verses add little substance to what Paul has said in the main body of his letter. But if that is our inclination, we are in for a surprise as we dig into these final verses because here Paul offers us a window into the heart of his ministry and his strategy for getting the gospel out to the ends of the earth.'

Alternatively, we could address a common misconception concerning Paul's approach to ministry: 'Many of us will picture Paul as something of a lone ranger, charging around the Mediterranean with heroic self-sufficiency, shrugging off the inconveniences of the occasional shipwreck or imprisonment. The reality could hardly be further from the stereotype. One scholar has gone through the New Testament counting up the number of friends and associates who join with Paul in his gospel work – and the tally reaches about 100 names. Gospel partners are absolutely fundamental to Paul's gospel work, as they must be to ours. And here in these final verses of 2 Timothy, Paul gives us a key insight into their value to him and his attitude toward them.'

Ideas for application

- Consider the story of Demas and be sobered. But for the grace of God, you and I could so easily go the way of Demas. Where are the affections of your heart set – on this world, or on the appearing of the Lord Jesus?

- Recognise the importance of investing in other potential leaders (as commended in 2:2) and then maintaining those relationships.

- Do not restrict your gospel horizon to your immediate surroundings. Think big-picture about the work of the gospel in your area and region and, indeed, throughout the world. See yourself as a gospel worker labouring alongside many others throughout the world. Pray for that broader work and support it in the ways that you can.

+ Do not put your trust in people; trust firmly in the sovereign God to sustain you, to further his work, and to deal justly with those who oppose the gospel.

+ Be concerned ultimately for the glory of God and not for your own reputation (which can be a danger if we do expand our horizon of concern and interest).

Suggestions for preaching

Paul gives us here a very personal window into the priorities of his ministry. It may not be easy to preach these verses consecutively, verse-by-verse, but we can draw some collected observations from them about Paul's priorities in ministry.

Four essentials for faithful and fruitful Gospel ministry:

1. A sustained investment in gospel partnerships

2. An enduring hunger for the word

3. A deep commitment to gospel proclamation

4. An absolute trust in the sovereignty of God

Suggestions for teaching

Questions to help understand the text

1. What is striking or surprising to you about the way Paul finishes his letter?

2. Paul spends much of his time in these final verses talking about specific people. What does this teach us about his outlook and priorities in ministry?

3. What has happened in Demas' heart and life (4:9-10)? How is he a contrast to Paul (4:8; note that the term translated 'longed for' in the NIV is literally 'loved' in the original)?

4. What is striking about Paul's request in verse 13? What does this teach us about his priorities?

5. What has kept Paul from despair as he has seen so many desert him and turn against him (4:14-18)?

6. Ultimately, what are the concerns and longings of Paul's heart (4:17-18)?

Questions to help apply the text

1. How is Demas a warning to us? How can we respond to that warning?

2. How can we value and invest in a broader network of Gospel partnerships, as Paul has? What practical steps can we take in this regard? What might be the fruit of such an investment?

3. Paul has a firm trust in the sovereign over-ruling of God as he considers the pain of opposition and the uncertainty of his own future. Where do we need to learn more deeply and apply more robustly this truth in our personal lives and in the lives of our churches?

4. Where are we tempted to work (even in the context of gospel service) for our own glory rather than God's? Where do we need to repent? How can we encourage one another to seek his glory above our own?

FURTHER READING

By far and away, the two books that were of most help to me in my study of 2 Timothy were the commentaries by John Stott (*The Message of 2 Timothy. The Bible Speaks Today.* Nottingham: Inter-Varsity Press, 1973) and J.N.D. Kelly (*The Pastoral Epistles I & II Timothy and Titus. Black's New Testament Commentaries.* London: A&C Black, 1963). It is no wonder that these works are modern classics; they are written with brevity and clarity and their treatment of the text is judicious and sane. Every preacher of 2 Timothy should aim to get hold of these, as should those who lead Bible studies on this book.

When first approaching 2 Timothy and seeking to find a way into the letter and the world it addressed, a very helpful guide is Christopher Green's short work (*Finishing the race: reading 2 Timothy today. Reading the Bible today.* Sydney: Aquila Press, 2000). Green adds much colour as he brings to life elements of the historical background to the letter (such as the grim reality of Paul's prison experience) and he offers a great deal of penetrating insight for application.

Beyond these works, preachers (especially) will want to have access to at least one or two more technical commentaries. The technical commentaries that I have used principally are the works by George W. Knight III (*The Pastoral Epistles. The New International Greek Testament Commentary*. Grand Rapids / Cambridge: Eerdmans, 1992), I.H. Marshall (*The Pastoral Epistles. International Critical Commentary*. London: T&T Clark, 1999) and William D. Mounce (*Pastoral Epistles, Word Biblical Commentary 46*. Nashville: Thomas Nelson, 2000). Each of these is a fine commentary and would be of great help in working through technical questions of exegesis. Marshall's ICC is perhaps the most accessible of the three in format (and Mounce's WBC the least). All three are worth the investment if your book budget stretches that far.

To these resources I would add the series of lectures given by Dick Lucas (*2 Timothy*. Address given at *The Proclamation Trust Evangelical Ministry Assembly*, 1986. Online: www.proctrust.org.uk) and Peter Adam (*2 Timothy – The Making of the Man of God*. Address given at *The Proclamation Trust Senior Ministers' Conference*, 2001. Online: www.proctrust.org.uk) on teaching and preaching 2 Timothy. These are overviews of 2 Timothy by seasoned preachers that go beyond exegesis to the doctrinal and pastoral implications of this letter to the contemporary people of God. They are available free online, and amply repay time invested listening to them.

PT RESOURCES

RESOURCES FOR PREACHERS AND BIBLE TEACHERS

PT Resources, a ministry of The Proclamation Trust, provides a range of multimedia resources for preachers and Bible teachers.

Teach the Bible Series (Christian Focus & PT Resources)
The Teaching the Bible Series, published jointly with Christian Focus Publications, is written by preachers, for preachers, and is specifically geared to the purpose of God's Word – its proclamation as living truth. Books in the series aim to help the reader move beyond simply understanding a text to communicating and applying it.

Current titles include: *Teaching Numbers, Teaching Isaiah, Teaching Amos, Teaching Matthew, Teaching John, Teaching Acts, Teaching Romans, Teaching Ephesians, Teaching 1 and 2 Thessalonians, Teaching 1 Timothy, Teaching 2 Timothy, Teaching 1 Peter, Bible Delight, Burning Hearts, Hearing the Spirit, Spirit of Truth, Teaching the Christian Hope, The Ministry Medical* and *The Priority of Preaching.*

Practical Preacher series
PT Resources publish a number of books addressing practical issues for preachers. These include *The Priority of Preaching, Bible Delight, Hearing the Spirit* and *The Ministry Medical*.

Online resources
We publish a large number of audio resources online, all of which are free to download. These are searchable through our website by speaker, date, topic and Bible book. The resources include:

- sermon series; examples of great preaching which not only demonstrate faithful principles but which will refresh and encourage the heart of the preacher

- instructions; audio which helps the teacher or preacher understand, open up and teach individual books of the Bible by getting to grips with their central message and purpose

- conference recordings; audio from all our conferences including the annual Evangelical Ministry Assembly. These talks discuss ministry and preaching issues.

An increasing number of resources are also available in video download form.

Online DVD
PT Resources have recently published online our collection of instructional videos by David Jackman. This material has been taught over the past 20 years on our PT Cornhill training course and around the world. It gives step by step instructions on handling each genre of biblical literature. There is also an online workbook. The videos are suitable

for preachers and those teaching the Bible in a variety of different contexts. Access to all the videos is free of charge.

The Proclaimer

Visit the Proclaimer blog for regular updates on matters to do with preaching. This is a short, punchy blog refreshed daily which is written by preachers and for preachers. It can be accessed via the PT website or through www.theproclaimer.org.uk.

'Teaching' titles from
Christian Focus and PT Resources

Teaching Numbers
ISBN 978-1-78191-156-3

Teaching Isaiah
ISBN 978-1-84550-565-3

Teaching Amos
ISBN 978-1-84550-142-6

Teaching Matthew
ISBN 978-1-84550-480-9

Teaching John
ISBN 978-1-85792-790-0

Teaching Acts
ISBN 978-1-84550-255-3

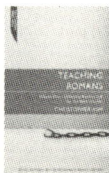

Teaching Romans (1)
ISBN 978-1-84550-455-7

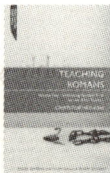

Teaching Romans (2)
ISBN 978-1-84550-456-4

Teaching Ephesians
ISBN 978-1-84550-684-1

Teaching 1 & 2 Thessalonians
ISBN 978-1-78191-325-3

Teaching 1 Timothy
ISBN 978-1-84550-808-1

Teaching 2 Timothy
ISBN 978-1-78191-389-5

Teaching 1 Peter
ISBN 978-1-84550-347-5

About the Proclamation Trust

We exist to promote church-based expository Bible ministry and especially to equip and encourage Biblical expository preachers because we recognise the primary role of preaching in God's sovereign purposes in the world through the local church.

Biblical (the message)
We believe the Bible is God's written Word and that, by the work of the Holy Spirit, as it is faithfully preached God's voice is truly heard.

Expository (the method)
Central to the preacher's task is correctly handling the Bible, seeking to discern the mind of the Spirit in the passage being expounded through prayerful study of the text in the light of its context in the biblical book and the Bible as a whole. This divine message must then be preached in dependence on the Holy Spirit to the minds, hearts and wills of the contemporary hearers.

Preachers (the messengers)
The public proclamation of God's Word by suitably gifted leaders is fundamental to a ministry that honours God, builds the church and reaches the world. God uses weak jars of clay in this task who need encouragement to persevere in their biblical convictions, ministry of God's Word and godly walk with Christ.

We achieve this through:

+ PT Cornhill: a one year full-time or two-year part-time church based training course

+ PT Conferences: offering practical encouragement for Bible preachers, teachers and ministers' wives

+ PT Resources: including books, online resources, the PT blog (www.theproclaimer.org.uk) and podcasts

Christian Focus Publications

Our mission statement –

STAYING FAITHFUL

In dependence upon God we seek to impact the world through literature faithful to His infallible Word, the Bible. Our aim is to ensure that the Lord Jesus Christ is presented as the only hope to obtain forgiveness of sin, live a useful life and look forward to heaven with Him.

Our books are published in four imprints:

CHRISTIAN
FOCUS

Popular works including biographies, commentaries, basic doctrine and Christian living.

CHRISTIAN
HERITAGE

Books representing some of the best material from the rich heritage of the church.

MENTOR

Books written at a level suitable for Bible College and seminary students, pastors, and other serious readers. The imprint includes commentaries, doctrinal studies, examination of current issues and church history.

CF4•K

Children's books for quality Bible teaching and for all age groups: Sunday school curriculum, puzzle and activity books; personal and family devotional titles, biographies and inspirational stories – because you are never too young to know Jesus!

Christian Focus Publications Ltd,
Geanies House, Fearn, Ross-shire,
IV20 1TW, Scotland, United Kingdom.
www.christianfocus.com